Ten-Minute Plays
Volume 6

from

Actors Theatre
of Louisville

Edited by
Tanya Palmer
Adrien-Alice Hansel
Steve Moulds

With a Foreword by Tanya Palmer

D1510287

A SAMUEL FRENCH ACTING EDITION

SAMUEL
FRENCH

FOUNDED 1830

SAMUELFRENCH.COM

MUSIC USE NOTE

Licensees are solely responsible for obtaining formal written permission from copyright owners to use copyrighted music in the performance of this play and are strongly cautioned to do so. If no such permission is obtained by the licensee, then the licensee must use only original music that the licensee owns and controls. Licensees are solely responsible and liable for all music clearances and shall indemnify the copyright owners of the play and their licensing agent, Samuel French, Inc., against any costs, expenses, losses and liabilities arising from the use of music by licensees.

IMPORTANT BILLING AND CREDIT REQUIREMENTS

All producers of *TEN-MINUTE PLAYS VOLUME 6 FROM ACTORS THEATRE OF LOUISVILLE must* give credit to the Author of the Play in all programs distributed in connection with performances of the Play, and in all instances in which the title of the Play appears for the purposes of advertising, publicizing or otherwise exploiting the Play and/or a production. The name of the Author *must* appear on a separate line on which no other name appears, immediately following the title and *must* appear in size of type not less than fifty percent of the size of the title type.

FOREWORD

There's nothing easy about writing a ten-minute play. Well, perhaps I should say there's nothing easy about writing a *good* ten-minute play. Sure, it's only ten pages, you could churn that out in an evening. But like the best poems or short stories, a good ten-minute play transcends its brevity, giving us a powerful insight, a stunning image, a hilarious story, a surprising event—all in the amount of time it takes to walk around the block. In this collection, you'll discover some of these short but remarkable gems—all distinct, filtered through the eyes of a diverse group of writers with their own way of translating their experience of the world. But while the subject matter and styles may be as numerous as the plays themselves, all these pieces share a few things in common: They get down to business quickly—when you've only got ten minutes, you can't ease into the story telling, you have to grab the audience and pull them in for a quick, wild ride. They pick their subjects wisely. It's hard to tackle an epic exploration of the Crimean Wars when you've got ten minutes, but you sure can tackle the brief but telling encounter between a soldier and his sergeant. And finally, they bring it all to a head. Not every ten-minute play is high drama—but here writers pack their transformations and revelations in tiny packages, and something is sure to happen in those ten minutes, whether it's a decision that will change a life or an afternoon.

At Actors Theatre of Louisville, we have no shortage of ten-minute plays. Since 1989, when the National Ten-Minute Play Contest first sprang into action, we've received upwards of 1200 plays every year from writers all across the country. We receive plays from college kids and grandmothers, poets and prisoners, and everyone in between. Not every play is a good one, but they all take a stab at capturing a truth about our lives and our world in ten short pages. The more we read, however, the more we realize how precious the ones that work truly are – those that grab us by the throats and demand our attention. We offer some of those to you here – a series of brief but powerful bursts of creative energy.

— *Tanya Palmer*

ABOUT ACTORS THEATRE OF LOUISVILLE

Actors Theatre of Louisville, the State Theatre of Kentucky, is internationally acclaimed as one of America's most consistently innovative nonprofit professional theatre companies. Founded in 1964, it has won a host of coveted awards and worldwide recognition for excellence. For 28 years it has been a major force in revitalizing American playwriting, with over 200 Actors-debuted scripts now in publication.

The annual Humana Festival of New American Plays is recognized as the premier event of its kind, and each spring draws producers, journalists, critics, playwrights and theatre lovers from around the world for a marathon of new works. More than 300 Humana Festival plays have been added to the active American stage repertoire. Three Pulitzer Prize winners have originated in the festival winners: *Dinner with Friends* by Donald Margulies, *Crimes of the Heart* by Beth Henley and *The Gin Game* by D. L. Coburn.

The thirty-seven year old theatre is the recipient of the most prestigious awards bestowed on a regional theatre: a special Tony Award for Distinguished Achievement, the James N. Vaughan Memorial Award for Exceptional Achievement and Contribution to the Development of Professional Theatre and the Margo Jones Award for the Encouragement of New Plays.

CONTENTS

ACKNOWLEDGEMENTS

In addition to all the playwrights whose plays are featured in this book, and the excellent staff at Samuel French, the editors wish to thank the following persons for their invaluable assistance in compiling this volume:

Erica Bradshaw
Rob Broderson
Erin Detrick
Michael Bigelow Dixon
Jennifer Hubbard
Jon Jory
Allison M. Leake
Dan LeFranc
Marc Masterson
Wendy McClellan
Meredith McDonough
Cathy Mellen
Jeffrey Rodgers
Alexander Speer
Sullivan Canaday White
Amy Wegener

AND

Beth Blickers
John Buzzetti
Val Day
Susan Shulman
Mark Christian Subias
Tina Howe

The Individuality
of Streetlamps

ANNA K. GORISCH

The Individuality of Streetlamps

by
Anna K. Gorisch

premiered in 2002 at the
Lion Theatre in New York, New York

Directed by Deborah Mathieu-Byers

<u>*Cast*</u>

Melissa	Rachiel Moriello
Andy	William Gregg Harris

Stage Manager: Jessica Pecharsky

CHARACTERS

MELISSA: A woman in her twenties.
ANDY: A man in his twenties.

SETTING

The front porch of a house.
A summer evening.
There is a porch swing, but it is not hanging.

The Individuality of Streetlamps

(At rise: MELISSA is sitting on the porch. She is sipping a beer, and is a little dressed up. ANDY walks up to the porch.)

ANDY. Hey there.

MELISSA. Hey. To what do I owe this honor?

ANDY. Oh, I just got off work, thought I'd drop by. What's with the outfit?

MELISSA. What do you mean?

ANDY. You look nice. Are you heading out soon?

MELISSA. No, I just got home from work.

ANDY. Is that what you wore to work?

MELISSA. Yeah? So?

ANDY. You wore that to a day-care center?

MELISSA. It's not a day-care center, it's a summer school for the arts.

ANDY. If you say so. It just doesn't seem like the right outfit to play with kids in.

MELISSA. I just wanted to look nice.

ANDY. You do. You look nice. You know I always loved that dress.

MELISSA. Yeah, I remember. *(Pause.)* You want a beer?

ANDY. Sure, thanks.

MELISSA. I'll get you one.

(She doesn't)

ANDY. So, how is the new job?

MELISSA. Good. Tiring. The kids are great. They wear me out. It doesn't pay enough. The usual.

ANDY. Good, I'm glad to hear it. At least I'm not the only one who's underappreciated.

MELISSA. Not hardly.

ANDY. What happened to the porch swing?

MELISSA. It fell.

ANDY. I can see that. Why?

(He goes over to inspect it.)

MELISSA. I don't know. Maybe I've put on weight.

ANDY. Christ, were you in it?

MELISSA. Unfortunately.

ANDY. Are you okay?

MELISSA. Yeah. I got a couple of bruises, but I'm okay.

ANDY. What were you doing?

MELISSA. I was swinging.

ANDY. Vigorously?

MELISSA. I guess.

ANDY. Well, whatever you were doing must have been intense. I don't think this can be fixed. You'll have to completely re-hang the thing.

MELISSA. I wouldn't begin to know how.

ANDY. Then it looks like you're swingless. I don't think I can fix it. These things aren't made for swinging. They're made for sitting.

MELISSA. I know. I don't want to talk about it, okay?

ANDY. Okay. *(Pause.)* What's with that streetlamp?

MELISSA. Hmmm? Oh, I don't know. It never really comes on and stays on. It just sort of flickers.

ANDY. Huh. I wonder why.

MELISSA. I have no idea, but it's been like that since I've lived here.

ANDY. Funny that I never noticed it before.

MELISSA. I guess your focus was elsewhere.

ANDY. Yeah, I guess it was.

(Pause.)

MELISSA. So, how's Amanda?

ANDY. She's good. She just got a new job downtown.

MELISSA. I bet it pays good.

ANDY. Unbelievable. She's got this huge office, big window, access to the company beach house in Florida, the works.

MELISSA. Must be nice. I can't complain, though. I have access to the company crayon box.

ANDY. Right on. And the kids are great, right?

MELISSA. Oh yeah. They're something. There's this one kid, Jason. He cracks me up. He's got this killer creative energy, and he's so focused. He's a lot of fun.

ANDY. What's his last name?

MELISSA. Stewart.

ANDY. Oh yeah. That's Barbara's kid.

MELISSA. Who's Barbara?

ANDY. Amanda's stepsister.

MELISSA. Well, hot damn, you're relatives.

ANDY. Yeah, in a sense. Barbara's brought her kids to a couple of family cookouts and stuff. Is he the one in middle school?

MELISSA. Yeah, he'll be twelve next month. I figure I'll make cupcakes or something. I hope I have one just like him someday.

ANDY. You really do like this kid.

MELISSA. Sure I do, he's great. He's so serious. Today he told me he would be leaving early. I asked him why. He said he had to go take care of something. He said it like he, I don't know, he had a meeting with his financial advisors or something. He's so cute.

ANDY. Oh my God.

MELISSA. What?

ANDY. I don't believe this.

MELISSA. What?

ANDY. You've got a crush on this kid.

MELISSA. Oh, for God's sake....

ANDY. You do, you have a crush on an eleven year old!

MELISSA. Oh, come on, he'll be twelve next month.

ANDY. He's not even a teenager.

MELISSA. I don't have a crush on him! That's completely ridiculous.

ANDY. Do you think about him when you're off work?

MELISSA. Yeah, sometimes.

ANDY. Got any pictures of him?

MELISSA. I got pictures of all the kids.

ANDY. Does he show up in your dreams?

MELISSA. Once I had a dream I was babysitting him, but so

what? This doesn't mean anything.

ANDY. Sounds like you've got all the classic signs.

MELISSA. He's just a great kid.

ANDY. Come on Mel, you can be honest with me. How long have you known me?

MELISSA. A long time.

ANDY. So?

MELISSA. Okay, so he makes me wish I was ten again. Things were so much simpler, you know?

ANDY. That's really sick.

MELISSA. It is not. I don't have fantasies about him for God's sake. He just reminds me of my childhood. He would have stolen my little heart, probably broken it. And I would have thought it was the end of the world. Funny how catastrophic things seemed when we were young. I don't know. He kind of likes me and I'm flattered. That's all.

ANDY. Is that why you wore the dress? To impress a preteen?

MELISSA. Can a woman not wear a dress without it having to be for a man?

ANDY. Calling him a man is a little inaccurate, don't you think?

MELISSA. Well, he's the most interesting and honest man I've come across in the last couple years.

ANDY. That's not fair, Mel.

MELISSA. God, Andy, I didn't mean you. Don't take it personally.

ANDY. How am I suppose to take it?

MELISSA. I don't know.

ANDY. I never lied to you.

MELISSA. No, you didn't. You just quite talking altogether.

ANDY. I didn't know what to say.

MELISSA. I know. I just wish I hadn't heard about the wedding from Marc. It would have been nice to have heard it from you.

ANDY. I feel shitty about that.

MELISSA. Ah, don't.

ANDY. I do though. The least I could have done was talk to you.

MELISSA. You could've invited me to the wedding.

ANDY. I didn't think that would be appropriate, considering the circumstances.

MELISSA. I suppose not..

ANDY. I miss you, though.

MELISSA. Do you now?

ANDY. Yeah, I mean, I was crazy about you. You're one of the most beautiful people I've ever known.

MELISSA. But you married Amanda.

ANDY. Yeah, yeah I did.

MELISSA. Well, she's great.

ANDY. Yes she is. But so are you.

MELISSA. So is Jason, but I don't expect I'll marry him. Not unless I come across him in ten or fifteen years and still think he's great.

ANDY. Hey, you never know.

MELISSA. You're a shit.

ANDY. Oooooh, ouch. That hurt.

MELISSA. Amanda's a lucky girl.

ANDY. Thank you. *(Pause.)* You want to go get some cheese-cake or something?

MELISSA. I better not. I gotta get up early. I need all my energy to keep up with those kids.

ANDY. Yeah, and you'll want to look your best.

MELISSA. I always want to look my best.

ANDY. You always do. *(He goes to kiss her, she backs away.)* Shit, Mel, I'm sorry.

MELISSA. That's alright.

ANDY. No, it's not. That wasn't fair.

MELISSA. Really, it's alright.

(Pause.)

ANDY. That streetlight is irritating as shit. It's distracting.

MELISSA. I used to think so. I don't know, though. He's just unique, you know? All those other streetlights are doing what is expected of them, what they're programmed to do, but he's just doing his own thing. I kind of admire his individuality.

ANDY. You're a nut, you know that?

MELISSA. I can't deny that.

ANDY. Well, I better get going. I have to stop by the store and pick up some coffee. We're out.

MELISSA. Yeah, you better. You're a bear in the morning without your coffee.

ANDY. Maybe next week we could grab some dinner.

MELISSA. Maybe. You know, last weekend I went out with some friends to that new jazz club for a few drinks. We had been there a couple of hours and I noticed that I was the only single person at the table. I wasn't even really a part of the conversation. I have no significant other to gripe about. I, of course, started thinking about you. Later that night, I found myself sitting in my porch swing with my headphones on, still thinking about you. It was just me, the music, and that damn streetlight. I kept hoping I would see your car, that you would stop by. The next thing I knew, the porch swing was hanging by one chain, and I was on the ground. I felt completely ridiculous. It was at that point that I knew you had really married Amanda, that you were never coming back. Apparently, the swing knew it all along. It was fed up with me sitting there, feeling sorry for myself and feeling alone, and if all I was gonna do was think about you, then it wouldn't have me. I will always miss you, but I am going to have to learn to live with that, because I cannot live with you. You can't come over and hang out on my porch, you have to come in or go away. You can't come in and I know that. I think you do too. That only leaves one option.

ANDY. Mel, for what it's worth ....

MELISSA. Which is not much ....

ANDY. Yeah, I know.

MELISSA. So, I'll see ya.

ANDY. Yeah. Okay. I'll see ya. Oh, and good luck with Jason. Let me know, I could maybe put in a good word for you.

MELISSA. Get out of here.

ANDY. Yeah, I will. I am.

(They look at each other for a moment. ANDY exits.)

MELISSA. Okay.

END OF THE PLAY

Swan Lake Calhoun

YEHUDA HYMAN

Swan Lake Calhoun

by
Yehuda Hyman

premiered in January, 2004 at
Actors Theatre of Louisville

Directed by Stephanie Cozart
Dramaturg: Dan LeFranc

Cast

Benny	Adam Suritz
Cig	Jesse Hooker
Lena	Lisa Benner

Scenic Designer: Brenda Ellis
Costume Designer: Andrea Scott
Lighting Designers: Amy McClure and Katie McCreary
Sound Designer: Bridget O'Connor
Properties Masters: Joe Cunningham and Anne Marie Werner
Stage Manager: Aaron Hurwitz
Assistant Stage Managers: Lisa Duwell and Kate Murphy
Fight Director: Brent Langdon

An earlier version premiered at the
Beast Festival Triangle Theatre, New York, NY

CHARACTERS

BENNY
CIG
LENA

SETTING

Winter. A frozen lake in Minnesota.
There is a hole in the ice.

Swan Lake Calhoun

(Two 20-year-olds, BENNY and CIG, are sitting on folding chairs on the ice-covered lake. They are ice fishing and drinking beer. CIG smokes. There are gunshots and then the sound of a flock of geese flying overhead, honking. The guys look up.)

BENNY. Hey, look. Swans!

CIG. Swans? Are you retarded? Those are geese.

BENNY. Geese? Are you sure?

CIG. Sure I'm sure. Honkin'. Shittin' all over everything. I hate those fuckin' birds.

BENNY. I dunno. They looked like swans to me.

CIG. That's the problem with you, Benny. You don't see life the way it is. You really must develop a fatal vision.

BENNY. Can't you look on the bright side for once?

CIG. There is no bright side. Look at us: ice fishin' on a Saturday night—it's tragic.

BENNY. We're not so bad off Cig, at least we got jobs.

CIG. White Castle is not a job, Benny, it's incarceration.

BENNY. Nah, c'mon. It's not that bad. We're gettin' that cappuccino machine next week 'n' everything. We're gonna be makin' lattes and stuff. It's gonna be really great.

CIG. In your dreams. *(He drains his can, crunches it and pulls another out of his cooler—offers it to BENNY.)* Grain Belt?

BENNY. Yuh, thanks.

(CIG gives the beer to BENNY and takes another one for himself.)

CIG. The thing is—I could die right now and so what? I mean, it's not like I'd really notice or anything.

BENNY. Yuh, I guess me too. Except—

19

CIG. Except what?

BENNY. I always wanted to go to Morocco.

CIG. Morocco?

BENNY. Yuh, I'd like to see the Casbah. I read about it—winding streets and stuff with hashish and spies and plush, colorful carpets. I'd like to see that before I die. What about you? Isn't there anything you'd like to see before you die?

CIG. No. I'm ready for the end. Bring it on. *(Suddenly his pole starts to jiggle.)* Whoa! Whoa, whoa. It's a big one. Whoa. Whoa, I said—Whoa!!!

(CIG struggles with the fish. It pulls him up off his chair towards the ice hole.)

BENNY. Cig, you're gonna fall in!

CIG. *(To the fish.)* Fuck you, Walleye, fuck you!

BENNY. Let it go!

CIG. I got it!

(He gets pulled and falls into the ice hole.)

BENNY. Cig!

CIG. Help!

BENNY. Cig!

CIG. I can't swim!

BENNY. Neither can I!

CIG. Shit! I'm dying!

BENNY. *(Runs around in a panic.)* Uhm! Uhm! Uhm!

(Then BENNY starts to run off.)

CIG. Where are you going?

BENNY. 911!

CIG. Don't leave me!

BENNY. *(Runs off screaming.)* Help!!!!!

CIG. *(Treading water—shivering.)* I can't fuckin' believe this, I'm actually gonna die. Please—God—or whatever, I didn't mean it—what I said before. I don't wanna die. Not really. Not yet. I was lying before. There is something I want. God this is so hard to say. Just once. I just once want to know ... *(He goes down. Comes back up.)* I just once want to know .... *(He goes down again. Comes up.)* Could you give me a minute? Ok? I just once want to know what it's like to love. To really feel it. What it's all about. That's all I'm askin' for. Just once?

(He goes down. Strange and wonderful music: Tchaikovsky. LENA, half woman/half goose, sails in on roller skates: feathers, wings, the whole bit. She wears a backpack. She circles around the ice hole—kneels down and pulls CIG out. He is unconscious. She holds his head in her arms, then leans down and kisses him. Nothing. She honks loudly. CIG wakes, startled.)

CIG. Huh?
LENA. *(She has a thick Ukrainian accent. She lets go of him and looks away.)* Taking off clothings, please.
CIG. What?
LENA. Taking off clothings, please to put these on.

(She takes clothes out of her backpack.)

CIG. I can't take my clothes off in front of you.
LENA. And why?
CIG. I don't even know you.
LENA. For goodness sake. I am Swan. You think I am interested? Take off before you freezing to death. *(She honks.)* Now!

(He stands up and pulls off clothes. LENA looks away. Hands him pants, etc. as he gets dressed.)

CIG. Uhm, excuse me?
LENA. Yes?
CIG. How come you can speak English and everything, if you're a goose.
LENA. *(She hisses at him.)* I am not goose.
CIG. I'm sorry, I just thought ....
LENA. I am swan. 100 per cent. Maybe I travel with gooses, maybe I am even looking like gooses but here, in my heart, I am having swan feelings, swan needs, swan desires. Don't call me goose.
CIG. I won't. I didn't understand ....
LENA. Yes, you don't understand nothing, you American boys

with your drinking and your cappuccinos. You don't know what is to suffer.

CIG. I'm sorry.

LENA. Never mind. Feel better?

CIG. Yeah. Much.

LENA. Well then, good luck Mister. I go.

(She starts to sail off.)

CIG. Wait!

LENA. What?

CIG. I don't even know your name.

LENA. Is Lena.

CIG. Lena? That's a pretty name. I'm Cig—Sigmund, really. Do you have a last name?

LENA. I can't remember. When the feathers came, I lost many memories.

CIG. When the feathers came?

LENA. I cannot say more.

(She starts to go off again.)

CIG. Wait, Lena. *(He runs to her. She stops.)* Please. Don't go. *(He takes her arm.)* Your feathers are really soft.

LENA. Yes. We manufacture natural emollient chemical—like lanolin but swanish. It's one of the pluses. *(He strokes her neck. She starts to preen—then pulls away.)* No more please.

CIG. And you smell nice too.

LENA. Is lavender. It grows over by Lake of the Isles where I live with goose boys. I rub it on myself every morning to hide the smell. I am so ashamed.

CIG. Lena, don't be ashamed. I—I like you.

LENA. Do you know what it is to live with gooses? I am trying all day to keep clean nest but is impossible. You see me like this but you cannot imagine what I was.

CIG. What were you?

LENA. You will not judge and condemn me? *(CIG shakes head.)* You swear?

CIG. I swear.

LENA. I was born in Ukraine—Kamyanets-Podolsky. There I am

having good life. Well, aside from industrial pollution, corruption and staggering unemployment resulting in massive emotional depressivities. Still, I have family and friends and fine achievable goal to be dental technician—but one day—I am seeing advertisement in newspaper—"We find you rich Americansky husband—No finder's fee." My old baba, she says to me "No, Lena, do not do this. Is bad—beware." But I am saying, "No, babutchka, I will make much money as mail-order bride and bring you to Minnesota where we will live in big fancy condominium with fully stocked sub-zero refrigerator and many other inessential but luxurious items." I dreamed I would be like fairy princess. Now look at me!

(She honks.)

CIG. What happened?

LENA. I am not reading fine print of contract. "If applicant not finding rich American husband after twenty days, phttt—you are goose!" Now you know truth —I am goose woman.

CIG. But that contract—that's illegal.

LENA. Yes, but what I do? Go on Court TV? Now I must only suffer. Suffer for all eternity, unless ....

CIG. What?

LENA. Unless someone could ... would ... no, is impossible.

CIG. Tell me, Lena, please.

LENA. If a man—will stay with me—in my nest—for one night —one whole night—and accept me as I am—with feathers and loud honkings and other various goose unpleasantries—then, in the morning, the curse will be lifted and I will once more again be—ah, I remember now—instead of Goose Woman I will be Lena Osmonova Odetteskaya, aspiring dental technician.

CIG. So, all I have to do is stay with you until morning and you'll become human again?

LENA. Yes.

CIG. Well, that sounds very do-able.

LENA. Really?!

CIG. Except that I have to be at work by 6 a.m.—'cause we're open for breakfast—at White Castle—we're open on Sunday—doesn't that suck?

LENA. *(Insecure.)* Ok, fine, no problem—I didn't think it would ....

(She starts to leave.)

CIG. No, you don't understand, I want to stay with you—Now—
all day—forever....
LENA. You do?
CIG. Yeah.
LENA. Really?
CIG. Yes, Lena. I—I—
LENA. What? Don't say it.
CIG. I love you!
LENA. No.
CIG. It's true.
LENA. Cig!
CIG. Lena!

(They run to each other. Except she slips and falls into the ice hole.)

LENA. Cig, help!

(He reaches in and tries to pull her out.)

CIG. Lena, take my arm!
LENA. It is so terribly cold!
CIG. Lena!
LENA. I'm dying, Cig.
CIG. No, Lena, no!
LENA. Yes, Cig, yes—it was inevitable. Happiness was brief but
memorable. Now it is over and I am being sucked into the vortex of
nothingness. Ah me!
CIG. I can save you!
LENA. No darling. Save yourself. Live. Live and tell the world
how once you loved me. Really loved me with much emotion and
lack of embarrassment. I'm going now.
CIG. No, it's not fair!
LENA. No, but it's beautifully tragic and that is the point. Live.
Love. Dasvedanya.

*(She pulls a feather out of herself and gives it to CIG. Then, she dis-
appears into the hole—only one graceful swanlike—er, goose-
like— arm visible—and then gone.)*

CIG. Lena!!!!!!!!!

(CIG reaches down. In despair, he collapses on the ice. Looks up. He gets up. Slowly starts to walk away. Looks back at ice hole— reaches for it. Music: A slow love song sung by a smoky-voiced singer. CIG comes back to the hole. He lights a cigarette and smokes it. He sits on the edge of the hole—his feet invisible in the hole. BENNY reenters with rope, a life vest and flippers.)

BENNY. Cig, you're alive!

CIG. *(He looks up.)* Love, Benny. For the first time in my life, love.

BENNY. When did this happen?

CIG. While you were gone. She was amazing.

(CIG shows the feather to BENNY.)

BENNY. She liked feathers?

CIG. She was ... a swan.

BENNY. I'm not getting something.

CIG. Alright, she was a goose. But to me she was a swan. Now what?

BENNY. Well—we could—now that you're not dying—we could stay and do more fishing.

CIG. Benny, don't you see what's happened?

BENNY. Well, you seem kind of upset.

CIG. It's Morocco, Benny. I've gone someplace and now there's no turning back.

BENNY. Sure there is.

CIG. No Cig, when you love someone—really love someone with all your heart—you're changed—forever.

BENNY. Well, you do look a little different.

(CIG lifts his feet out of the ice hole. He's now wearing "swan" roller skates. He gets up. He honks. He starts to skate around—flapping his wings with grace and honking.)

BENNY. Cig, cut it out, you're scarin' me!

CIG. Don't be scared Benny. It's beautiful.

BENNY. What is?

CIG. It's soft as lanolin, sweet as lavender and it has wings. Tell them, Benny. Tell them all!

BENNY. Tell them what?

CIG. Love, Benny. Love has wings!

(CIG skates off as the sun comes through.)

END OF THE PLAY

Kuwait

VINCENT DELANEY

Kuwait

by
Vincent Delaney

premiered in April, 2004 at the
Humana Festival of New American Plays

Directed by Meredith McDonough
Dramaturg: Steve Moulds

Cast

Rachel	Julie Jesneck
Kelsey	Asa Somers
Miles	Stephen Thorne

Scenic Designer: Paul Owen
Costume Designer: John P. White
Lighting Designer: Paul Werner
Sound Designer: Benjamin Marcum
Properties Designer: Doc Manning
Stage Manager: Debra A. Freeman
Assistant Stage Managers: Michael Domue and Brady Ellen Poole

CHARACTERS

RACHEL: a journalist.
KELSEY: a soldier.
MILES: an escort.

SETTING

A hotel room in the Middle East.

Kuwait

(A hotel room in the Middle East. A single bed, table and chair, bath-
    room to the side, a window downstage which looks out over a
    city. Several bland desert prints on the wall.
The door bursts open. RACHEL stumbles in, blindfolded and hand-
    cuffed. She's followed by KELSEY, in uniform, who stands in the
    door, holding her travel bag.)

RACHEL. I'm suing, I'm suing, you are so sued. You personally, whoever you are, and I know you hear me, you have got legal
bills like you can't imagine. Go ask for a raise, because you owe by
the minute. *(She collides with the bed.)* Is this a bed? All right. My
driver knows I left this morning, because he was with me. He is
aware, do you hear me, he is most certainly aware that I've been kid-
napped and he will be looking, I said he will be looking for me!
(KELSEY shuts the door. It clicks softly. She hears it.) My name is
Rachel Cayman, I'm a correspondent for the *Times* and an American
citizen. Hello? If anyone else is here please say something. My paper
will offer a reward, in dollars. *(KELSEY unpacks Rachel's bag. He
lays out her equipment: camera, tape recorder, notebooks, purse.)* Is
that my bag? Are you in my bag? Son of a bitch. I know we're back
in Saudi, okay? I timed it. Ten thousand five hundred seconds. One
hundred eighty minutes. Three God damn hours in the back of your
non-air conditioned Jeep. Do you know who I am? I am going to own
you, soldier.

KELSEY. Unescorted pool reporters are not allowed in the combat zone.

RACHEL. It speaks. They must have raised the bar for recruits.
(KELSEY unsnaps her camera case.) Don't touch that. Don't. All
right, I snuck into the zone. I admit it. I broke the rules. I took pictures
of dirt. I interviewed a camel. There's nothing on my film but sand

29

dunes. Wait. Asshole! *(He pulls the film out of her camera, unravels it.)* They teach you this at boot camp? You're very good at it.

KELSEY. Per the standing orders regarding breach of the combat zone, you will be detained here for twenty-four hours.

RACHEL. What the fuck are you talking about? The war will be over in twenty-four hours.

KELSEY. At the end of that time, you will be released to the custody of your military escort.

RACHEL. Hey asshole, did you hear me?

(She lurches toward him.)

KELSEY. Please desist. I don't wish to use restraints.

RACHEL. Oh, but they'd be so much fun. *(She sits. He reads through her journals.)* So you pulled guard duty. Poor kid. If I were you I'd be pissed. Maybe you'd like to talk about it. I've got time. *(He tears pages out of her journals, sets them aside.)* That's my notebook, isn't it? Well done. You've arrived, soldier. All those pushups paid off. Here you are, on the frontline, taking on a journalist. Fair warning, I know yoga. Isn't the blindfold kind of melodramatic? Or is this bedspread classified?

KELSEY. The rules of engagement provide for the use of necessary correctives.

RACHEL. Could you say that again?

KELSEY. The rules of engagement provide for the use of necessary correctives.

RACHEL. Thank you. Now tell me what the fuck it means.

KELSEY. You were issued the directives regarding press access. You are advised to read them.

RACHEL. Okay, hand me my copy. *(He dumps her purse out.)* Help yourself. You smoke? That sounds like a yes. Pack of Marlboros in my purse. Go ahead.

KELSEY. I don't smoke.

RACHEL. Come on soldier, got to do better than that. I hear nicotine in your voice. What you gonna do, you get captured? *(Accent.)* American Yankee, when marches the Great Satan on our cities? *(Mimics KELSEY.)* I don't know. But I swear I don't smoke. *(Herself.)* Just trying to improve your mood. *(He pulls out a mini-tape recorder, pops out the cassette.)* These cuffs should be tighter. I'm not even getting chafed here.

KELSEY. What's on this cassette?

RACHEL. Motley Crüe. Serious, I'm a metal freak. Play it if you don't believe me. Play it! *(He sets the tape down.)* Do you even care that I'll be fired for this?

KELSEY. Sorry if the war is inconveniencing you.

RACHEL. Could that have been irony? Did I just hear sharp, caustic sarcasm from the mouth of my military keeper? Do that again. *(KELSEY looks at her cigarettes.)* Go ahead, light up. *(Startled, he goes to her and checks her blindfold.)* Don't worry, it's pitch black in here. I just smelt the craving.

KELSEY. If you require any special considerations please make a request to the duty officer.

RACHEL. I have a request.

KELSEY. Sanitary facilities are provided. Upon request, a female officer will escort you to them.

RACHEL. I have a request.

KELSEY. Special dietary needs may not be met.

RACHEL. I have a request.

KELSEY. What is your request?

RACHEL. Tell me your name, rank and serial number. *(Silence.)* In that case I'll just sit here and picture you. I'm guessing five foot six. That's below minimum. Let's say five six and a half. Five seven in boots. Extremely broad. Squat body. Arms won't fully extend. All that muscle mass. Completely bald on top. Sort of a Bruce Willis, Sylvester Stallone, Wallace Shawn hybrid. Am I close? *(He lights a cigarette.)* Guess I nailed it. Make yourself at home, soldier. *(He watches her, smoking.)* So how big's your gun? You mean you don't have one? I am so sorry. If you did have one, I'm sure it would be a big one. What you do to get stuck with me? Must have been bad. Let me guess. Panic under fire? Oops, shouldn't have said that. *(He smokes.)* Where's mine?

KELSEY. Smoking is not permitted.

RACHEL. Won't tell if you don't. Give me a drink. Piece of shit.

KELSEY. That's not how we ask.

RACHEL. Do you know who I am? Do you know how much I make? Do you know how utterly insignificant you are, right here, right now? Do you? *(Beat.)* May I have a drink, please? *(KELSEY takes a cup to the sink.)* No, a drink. It's been a bitch of a day. I want a beer.

KELSEY. A beer.

RACHEL. Don't tell me there's no beer.

KELSEY. There's no beer.

RACHEL. Oh come on. You are old enough. Aren't you? *(Beat.)* This could be your first beer. Ever. A beautiful thing.

KELSEY. The consumption of beer is not permitted.

RACHEL. Okay, how about a martini? You don't have a sense of humor, do you?

KELSEY. If you need anything, please ring the bell.

RACHEL. What bell? Wait, that was humor. That was very nice.

KELSEY. This isn't Motley Crüe. Is it?

RACHEL. Would I lie to you? *(KELSEY turns the tape on. Heavy metal music roars forth. RACHEL busts out laughing.)* I got him! I got him! I love it. *(He puts the cigarette out, paces.)* Sorry. Motley Crüe just really gets me off. That heavy metal beat, sounds like a Scud missile. BOOM da da BOOM da da BOOM BOOM BOOM, primal, like gutting the enemy with a brick. Maybe that's what you lack, soldier. Little more AC/DC in your life. Get your hormone level up. Make those little jewels finally drop down. Let's pick a band for you. Slayer? Too masculine. Prong? Doesn't really fit, does it? I know: Anthrax. That wasn't funny. Social gaffe, social gaffe. Open a window, I'm hot.

KELSEY. There's no window.

RACHEL. No window?

KELSEY. We're underground.

RACHEL. We're in a hotel room.

KELSEY. It's a bunker.

RACHEL. A what?

KELSEY. This is an interrogation facility.

RACHEL. Interrogation? What, torture?

KELSEY. We wouldn't do that, would we?

RACHEL. Oh my God, I got the one with a sense of humor. *(KELSEY goes in the bathroom, breathes deep, washes his hands.)* What are the chances of getting this thing off my face?

KELSEY. Not good.

RACHEL. National security?

KELSEY. No. I just don't feel like it.

RACHEL. We are getting familiar, aren't we? Hey! Asshole! Even prisoners of war have rights!

(He returns, holding his towel.)

KELSEY. You're not a prisoner of war.

RACHEL. What do you expect me to do in here?

KELSEY. Enjoy the view.

RACHEL. You chicken shit babysitter. Just 'cause they don't want your ass holding a rifle, don't keep me down! I'll take fire! I won't cower on guard duty! I know you hear me, you coward! I have a story to file, you piece of shit underage no balls babysitter!

(She leaps up. He comes to her, graceful, swift, and takes her back to the bed. He straddles her, whispers his speech right in her ear.)

KELSEY. It's brick in here. Floor to ceiling. So dark you can't hardly see. Scratches on the wall. Long ones, from fingers, broken nails. Stains, blotches all over. One just by your head. Up on the ceiling, that's a blood spatter. Big one, spreading out, dried up. Here, feel it. *(He takes her hand, brushes the wall.)* That's a Polaroid. Taped on the wall. All around you, on the walls, pictures, couple hundred. Souvenirs, leftovers. Guys bleeding, guys dead, guys getting shocked. Guys getting drowned. We use a basin. Just a little one, maybe half gallon. Take a long while, drown a guy that way. Shove his face in, thirty seconds, let him breathe. Shove him back in, sixty seconds … let him breathe. Make him hope. Think he might live. Then we start talking to you. How's it feel? What you think about, in the water? You see death in there? You see him looking up at you, going for your eyes? Shove your face in … in … and maybe … you don't … get to breathe any more.

(KELSEY flicks his towel at her.)

RACHEL. Why are you doing this to me? *(KELSEY recovers, gets away from her, takes his gun out, breaks it down.)* I want the female escort.

KELSEY. You don't have to go.

RACHEL. Yes I do, I have to go.

KELSEY. No you don't.

RACHEL. I have to go.

KELSEY. You're faking.

RACHEL. I know my own bodily functions!

KELSEY. No.

RACHEL. How can you tell?

KELSEY. You learn.

RACHEL. Is it a tone of voice thing?

KELSEY. You learn.

RACHEL. My driver is looking for me.

KELSEY. Your driver is dead.

RACHEL. Dead.

KELSEY. Land mine. On the way back.

RACHEL. He's dead?

KELSEY. Things happen.

RACHEL. No.

KELSEY. How much information do you really want?

(Silence.)

RACHEL. So you do have a gun.

(He steps to her, holding his gun.)

KELSEY. Not everybody gets interrogated. Maybe you're sound asleep. In the dark, in a trench. Can't hear a thing. Like a tomb in there. Air is warm, heavy, desert air. And we bring a bulldozer, right over you, and do we wake you first? Do we say, get out, leave your weapon, just get out and walk away, we don't want you, we know you didn't choose this, we know you're a person? No, we bury you. Under all that sand. Not crushed, buried. *(He pulls a blanket up and drapes it over her.)* Still alive. Maybe you hear it, for a second, that trembling, and then we punch through the berm, we move the sand and you're under it. Press on your chest, press on your face, all that sand, like an avalanche, but warm, trickling, sliding like snakes, can't even open your eyes and if you did what could you see? What could you see? On your head, on your eyes. So quiet now. Twenty feet of sand, trickling in your ears, still breathing, so quiet. What can you see? You're going to live a few more seconds, you can hope, no reason not to hope, and what do you hope for? What do you want now? Tell me what you want now!

(RACHEL screams. MILES enters.)

MILES. Okay, this looks cozy. Let me guess, charades. She too cold? Ma'am, are you too cold? You want to take that off her, please, Kelsey? *(KELSEY pulls the blanket off RACHEL.)* Blindfolded? Whose bright idea was that? I guess the bedspread's classified. How you doing in there?

RACHEL. Okay.

MILES. Is there a reason you're all tied up?

RACHEL. I've been a bad girl.

MILES. Damn right you have, Rachel. Sure gave me the slip. Wraps her face like a Bedouin and saunters right past me in the lobby. Right out into the desert. Takes a driver, and off she goes. Without me. Really fucked me over with my C.O. Guess what my punishment is?

RACHEL. More time with me.

MILES. You ought to enlist, you're sharp.

RACHEL. Where am I?

MILES. Where do you think you are? Let's get this shit off you. *(MILES pulls off her blindfold. She takes him in, the room, the walls, and finally KELSEY, who stands to the side, looking away. Silence.)* Am I missing something here?

RACHEL. When we went in, did we bury any Iraqis?

MILES. Bury Iraqis?

RACHEL. In the sand. With bulldozers. Did we bury any of them alive?

MILES. I'd say the cuffs are a tad melodramatic, wouldn't you?

RACHEL. I asked you a question.

MILES. Let's get you decent. Key, please. *(MILES holds out his hand, but KELSEY ignores him, goes and uncuffs RACHEL. He steps back. They stare at each other.)* Somebody want to tell me what's going on here? Has this soldier behaved in an inappropriate manner?

RACHEL. Not at all.

MILES. So, good news is, your paper pitched a holy diva, and now you're back down in the lobby, full credential. Bad news is, I'm down there with you. With my career fucked. So let's go.

RACHEL. No.

MILES. No?

RACHEL. Go on back, Miles. Kelsey will bring me to the lobby.

MILES. I'm your escort. It's my job.

RACHEL. He'll bring me. *(MILES stares at them both, starts to speak, then gives up and exits. A beat.)* Do you want to talk about it?

*(KELSEY looks away, then at her. He sits.
Blackout.)*

END OF THE PLAY

Foul Territory

CRAIG WRIGHT

Foul Territory

by
Craig Wright

*premiered in April, 2004 at the
Humana Festival of New American Plays*

Directed by Sturgis Warner
Dramaturg: Steve Moulds

Cast

Ruth	Russell Arden Koplin
Owen	Jesse Lenat

Scenic Designer: Paul Owen
Costume Designer: Andrea Scott
Lighting Designer: Paul Werner
Sound Designer: Benjamin Marcum
Properties Designer: Doc Manning
Stage Manager: Debra A. Freeman
Assistant Stage Managers: Michael Domue and Brady Ellen Poole
Ball Handler: Sturgis Warner

CHARACTERS

OWEN: A man in his 30's or 40's.
RUTH: A woman in her 30's or 40's.

SETTING

Yankee Stadium.

Foul Territory

(The scene is a row of far left-field seats at Yankee Stadium. OWEN is seated next to RUTH. Throughout the scene we can hear a baseball game in progress: the distant drone of the announcer giving the play-by-play, the general crowd roar, and the periodic crack of the bat hitting the ball. OWEN and RUTH are both eating popcorn or peanuts.)

RUTH. I think they're gonna do it this year, Owen. I can feel it. They're going all the way. Three months from now, mark my words, it's the World Series, and we'll be sitting here winnin' it.... *(She eats a mouthful of popcorn, then finishes her thought with her mouth full.)* Mark my words. *(Another big mouthful—and she turns to OWEN—)* Don'tcha think? *(—to catch him eyeing her with pity.)* What? What are you looking at? What?

OWEN. *(After a beat, pityingly.)* You're so brave.

RUTH. Gimme a break.

OWEN. No, I mean it, Ruth, you are—

RUTH. Because I think the *Yankees* have a chance? It doesn't take a genius—

OWEN. No, to be out here like this, like you are.

RUTH. At the game?

OWEN. At the game, at the whole thing! *(We hear the crack of the bat hitting the ball.)* To be getting back on your feet the way you're getting—after what Tom did to you—you're so sweet and brave— *(He eats a single piece of popcorn, gazing at her. She tracks the approaching ball with her eyes.)* —so sweet and brave.

RUTH. Stop it.

OWEN. No, I mean it, you're like, straight outta Laura Ingalls Wilder, I'm so proud of you, to bounce back like this. After Monty left me— *(A ball sails in and cracks OWEN loudly on the head.)* OW!

RUTH. Oh God! Oh God, Owen, are you alright? Oh God!

OWEN. *(Holding his head.)* I'm fine, I'm fine—

RUTH. Didn't you see that coming?

OWEN. Yeah, I, I kinda did ....

RUTH. It was coming right at you—

OWEN. I know—

RUTH. Oh my God ... do you need anything? Ice, or—

OWEN. No—

RUTH. Should we take you to First Aid or something?

OWEN. No, I'm fine! I'm good. Really. Just watch your game, honey. Enjoy yourself. It's your night. It's your night.

RUTH. You're sure?

OWEN. Yes—

RUTH. Because we can go, really—

OWEN. *(Still rocking, in terrible pain.)* No, I'm shakin' it off. I'm a trooper. I'm fine.

RUTH. *(Double-checking.)* You're absolutely sure?

OWEN. Yes.

RUTH. *(Doubtfully.)* Ok. Ok. You're sure you're alright?

OWEN. Yep. Par for the course. I'm fine.

RUTH. Ok. Ok. *(She settles back into watching the game. A moment passes. Something catches her eye.)* Did you see that?

OWEN. No, what?

RUTH. He balked. *(To the field.)* Stay on the rubber! *(After a long beat.)* Look, he did it again— *(She stands and screams at the field.)* Stay on the rubber! This isn't Cuba, pal! *(To OWEN.)* Do you see what I'm talkin' about?

OWEN. *(Still rubbing his head.)* No, I—I missed it—

RUTH. He balks, like every third pitch, this guy, and no one calls it! No one ever calls it! *(Amazed.)* Jesus. *(She sits back down, eats some popcorn.)* What's the point of having a rule if no one's gonna call it?

(We hear the crack of the bat hitting the ball. A moment passes.)

OWEN. Have you heard from him? At all?

RUTH. I don't want to talk about it—

OWEN. Wouldja take him back?

RUTH. No! *(She starts tracking the approaching ball.)* You don't get it, Owen, Tom Scintilla leaving me is the *best thing* that ever could have happened—to me or the kids—

OWEN. But you miss him—

RUTH. I don't—

OWEN. Oh, come on, you miss him and you want him back, just admit it. When Monty left me— *(The ball sails in and hits him hard in the face.)* OW!!

RUTH. *(Angry and concerned.)* Owen, move!!

(Blood sprays from his nose. He clutches it in agony.)

OWEN. When?

RUTH. *When you see the ball coming!* God! Are you alright? Is anything broken?

OWEN. No, it just … it just kinda … *hurts….* *(She pulls a napkin from her popcorn container and anxiously dabs his nose, trying to soak up some of the blood.)* Ow, ow, ow….

RUTH. *(After a beat, with one eye on the game.)* So you saw that coming?

OWEN. Of course!

RUTH. So why didn't you *move*?

OWEN. What would be the point?

RUTH. What the hell does that mean? Jesus— *(She suddenly stands up and screams at the field.)* Would someone please nail this guy's feet to the motherfuckin' rubber or make the call??? Jesus Christ! (She sits back down, annoyed with the game.) I mean, this guy's not gonna cost us the game, but *shit!* (A moment passes as she eats some popcorn and looks at OWEN.) So what do you mean, "what would be the point?"

OWEN. It doesn't matter—

RUTH. Sure it does—

OWEN. No, you're enjoying the game—

RUTH. No, tell me! I've been going to baseball games for thirty-five years, Owen, I never caught a foul ball once and I just saw you get hit twice in one game!

OWEN. That's life—

RUTH. No, it's not life, it's fuckin' weird! *(Then, responding approvingly to the field.)* There! Thank you! *(To OWEN.)* Do you realize, now, with __*(Fill in player's name)*__ on base, if __*(Fill in player's name)*__ hits a home run, it's over, right?

OWEN. Yeah—

RUTH. This is a good game—

OWEN. When I got hit in the face with a baseball the *first* time—

RUTH. *(Caught off guard.)* How many times have you been hit?

OWEN. I don't know, a lot.

RUTH. You never told me this—

OWEN. It never came up—we never went to a game—

RUTH. I guess you're right—

OWEN. —the first time I was eleven years old, trying to catch a pop fly in the street—

RUTH. You played baseball?

OWEN. I know, it's unlikely—

RUTH. It's mega-unlikely—

OWEN. Well, I did, and this kid hit a pop fly and I must have misjudged or something, the important part is BANG, I got hit right between the eyes.

RUTH. Ouch.

OWEN. Yeah. There was blood everywhere, my eyes were swollen shut—

RUTH. God—

OWEN. Yeah, and I got totally spooked.

(He blows his nose and the napkin fills with blood.)

RUTH. Are you sure you're alright?

OWEN. Yeah, I just feel a little … a little faint, anyway, a couple days later, I was at a baseball game for my school—not even playing, I was just doing stats, because my vision was still a little screwed up, and Jonny Blank hit a high foul and I freaked out. Everyone else was just sitting there, and I'm screaming, running around like a bee is chasing me and I'm ALREADY crying and I finally find the spot where I'm safe and I crouch down and cover my ears, but then I hear somebody catch it, so I look up and BANG, it hits me in the face!

RUTH. Oh my God!

OWEN. I know!

RUTH. What are the chances?

OWEN. Very high, obviously—

RUTH. *(Affirmatively.)* I guess—

OWEN. Anyway, I spent the next week in the hospital.

RUTH. The hospital?

OWEN. Kind of a ... mental hospital—

RUTH. Oh—

OWEN. —and when I got out, my father, my beloved father whom I must have generated in my previous life in some evil DUNGEON, fabricated him from trash like some Golem, you know, to torture me later in case I forgot what was true about GOD, my beloved father decided to take me to a baseball game. He told me I had to get back on the horse. I cried the whole way in the car, "Don't take me. Turn around, I want to go home." He didn't care. We got to the game and lo and behold—

RUTH. You got hit—

OWEN. No. Nothing happened. *(After a beat.)* For eight innings.

RUTH. Oh no—

OWEN. And then Lou Piniella hit a high foul into the stands, and my father said "Just sit still," and I did—for two seconds—and then I RAN up the stairs into an empty row that looked safe and BANG, it caught me right in the ear!

RUTH. No!

OWEN. Yes! I still can't hear anything in this ear! I point this ear at something, I hear the ocean. MAYBE.

RUTH. That's amazing.

OWEN. We can't run, Ruth, that's my point. Whether it's baseballs or heartbreak, whether it's your Tom or my Monty, there's no escaping it. Life is going to destroy us. It's going to. Letting it happen is the only freedom we have.

RUTH. But Owen, that's absurd—

OWEN. It's the truth!

RUTH. But Owen, I'm happier now than I've been in ten years! The house is clean, all of Tom's stupid model train stuff is outta there; the kids are doing better in school; Carla Kendall is setting me up next week with a really nice guy—

OWEN. *(Doubtful.)* Oh, right—

RUTH. He sounds really sweet, he's a personal trainer—

OWEN. Sure he is—

RUTH. I think things are really looking up!

OWEN. And I think you're kidding yourself! I think you're seriously kidding yourself. *(We hear a loud crack of the bat hitting the ball. Fatalistically.)* See, here it comes again.

(RUTH stands up.)

RUTH. Catch it!

OWEN. No, there's no point!

RUTH. Owen, stand up, put out your hands and catch it!

(She pulls him up.)

OWEN. But if I reach here, the ball goes there, Ruth, wherever I reach is where it won't be!

RUTH. That can't be true!

OWEN. *(Indicating his bloody nose.)* Look at me, Ruth, if anything's true, it's true, I know my own life——

RUTH. Put out your hands! *(She puts out his hands.)* Now keep your eyes open, keep your eye on the ball, and catch it!

OWEN. Ok, I'll try!

RUTH. Here it comes ... here it comes ... here it comes.... *(Their eyes track the incoming ball. OWEN's ready to catch it. Boom, it hits OWEN in the face with a loud smack. He falls over, clutching his face in quiet agony. RUTH doesn't react in horror this time. She just looks down at him. After a long beat.)* But see, aren't you glad you made the *effort*?

OWEN. *(From down on the ground, curled up in pain, after a beat.)* Yeah, I'm glad.

RUTH. You'll get the next one. Just tell yourself, "I'll get the next one."

OWEN. "I'll get the next one."

RUTH. You can't lose hope, Owen. That's what I tell the kids. We can't lose hope. It's all we've got. *(She sits down, eats some popcorn, watches the field with interest.)* I really think we have a shot this year. I think we're really gonna go all the way.

END OF THE PLAY

Creep

JAMES CHRISTY

Creep

by
James Christy

premiered in August, 2000 at
Actors Theatre of Louisville

Directed by Barrett Cooper
Dramaturg: Emily Roderer

<u>*Cast*</u>

Anne	Kelly Fagan
Hoover	Drew Hirshfield

Costume Designer: Julianne Johnson
Lighting Designer: Tony Penna
Sound Designer: Dave Preston
Properties Designer: Doc Manning
Stage Manager: Emily Brauer

Creep *is part of a full-length play called* **Never Tell**,
which premiered at the New York Fringe Festival in 2004.

CHARACTERS

ANNE
HOOVER

SETTING

A party in Brooklyn.

Creep

(ANNE is on a cell phone at a party. On the other side of the stage
HOOVER sits on a couch, his arm draped over the side holding a
beer. He is eavesdropping.)

ANNE. You think I'm enjoying myself? My jacket is on and I've
been giving her dirty looks since we got here.... No, not right this
second, I told her I'd give her a half-hour, she's got ten more minutes.
I don't know, she thinks if I leave without her it'll be too forward.
(Confidentially.) She's worse than usual tonight ... kissing this guy's
ass and laughing at things that aren't funny ... it's the same shit.... I
know ... I know, and then she wonders why they make her miserable.... *(Looking at a spot across the room.)* Boring. Terminally boring.... Not really, but you don't have to talk to him, you can just tell,
he's got it all over his face. All over his clothes. He's just mediocre,
you know, he can't help it. *(She turns around and sees HOOVER*
looking at her.) Okay, I have to go. Soon. Love you too.

(She hangs up. HOOVER looks at her for a beat then looks away.)

HOOVER. Who do you know?
ANNE. What?
HOOVER. Who do you know who do you know who do you
know? Here, at the party, who do you know?
ANNE. No one. I'm, uh, a friend of a friend. I'm really just wait-
ing for someone.
HOOVER. Uh huh. Do you want me to introduce you around? I
can introduce you to some people.
ANNE. No thanks, I'm not really feeling so well.
HOOVER. Really? Huh. I'm sorry to hear that.
ANNE. I'm fine, I'm just not feeling too social.

(Pause.)

> HOOVER. You see that guy over there?
> ANNE. Which one, the guy with the purple jacket?
> HOOVER. No not that fuck, the guy by the sink.
> ANNE. Yeah?
> HOOVER. He's got Kurt Cobain's pancreas.
> ANNE. What?
> HOOVER. *(As he swigs his beer.)* No shit. Cobain's pancreas.
> ANNE. Why?

HOOVER. I don't know, he's always had this fucked up pancreas, some genetic thing, and he needed a new one, and for a long time he was on this waiting list because they're hard to come by and he wasn't, like, on the brink or anything. But one day his doctor called him up and told him to bring his ass in for surgery. He didn't know it was Cobain's pancreas until like two days later. He hadn't even heard he was dead yet, this candy striper chick comes up to him when he comes out of it and goes, "Dude, you're so lucky, you got Kurt's pancreas." And he's like, what the fuck, and she's like "yeah, don't tell anyone I told you, I could get in trouble, it's supposed to be confidential." *(Beat.)* Can you imagine that shit? To wake up and find out A that Cobain's dead, and B that you've got his fuckin' pancreas? Jesus Christ.

ANNE. But wouldn't it be ... I mean, he was like a heroin addict wasn't he? Can they just give them out when they're—

HOOVER. That's what I thought, but it was cool. Apparently his liver and his stomach linings were all fucked up but his pancreas was fine.

ANNE. And he's okay now? Your friend?

HOOVER. He's not my friend. I think he's kind of a dick actually, but yeah he's alright. He's not supposed to drink anymore, but he does anyway and nothing's happened to him yet. Can't listen to Nirvana though.

ANNE. Jesus.

HOOVER. And you see that guy playing the video game?

ANNE. Yeah.

HOOVER. He's this gamer freak. That's all he does. He never leaves his apartment. He's only here because somebody made this homemade video game he wanted to check out.

ANNE. That's, very sad.

HOOVER. Like four years ago he was totally broke, about to be evicted from his apartment 'cause he didn't have a job. And still all he did was play video games. He was like pathological. Finally some newspaper does an article about how all this guy does is play video games and he knows like every one ever made or whatever. And then this gaming company reads about it and hires him to just sit on his ass and play video games all day as a "consultant." And they pay him a buttload of money just to tell them what he thinks of these games. That's it.

ANNE. *(Shaking her head.)* The American dream.

HOOVER. Yeah, but the weird thing is that he has all this cash now, he's like a millionaire from this job. But he still lives the same way, in the same shitty apartment—

ANNE. *(Under her breath.)* Wears the same shitty clothes ....

HOOVER. He still acts like he has no money because he feels that with money he'll lose his identity. Without money he was a loser, he was used to that, he knew what it was, he did it well. Now if he starts to enjoy his money he thinks he has this huge potential to fuck it up somehow, to lose it or get it ripped off, you know? It makes sense when you think about it.

(Beat. She looks at him, he looks down.)

ANNE. No, no it doesn't make sense. That makes no sense. In fact, that sounds like bullshit. *(He tries to contain a smile.)* It's all bullshit, isn't it? That guy doesn't have Kurt Cobain's pancreas, and that guy is no millionaire. *(He laughs.)* What is your problem?

HOOVER. So, what's your problem with Liz?

ANNE. What? How do you know her name?

HOOVER. I don't think he looks boring, he seems cool enough to me.

ANNE. You heard that? You were listening to me?

HOOVER. And as for kissing his ass I think she's just being polite, you know. There's nothing wrong with that.

ANNE. So what you've been fucking spying on me?

HOOVER. To me it looks like you're jealous.

ANNE. Jealous of Liz? Jealous of Liz because she's talking to some zombie broker from New Canaan?

HOOVER. So why are you so angry with her?

ANNE. First of all I'm not, second of all if I was it's just because I'm stuck here in this hole talking to you when there's somewhere I'm supposed to be.

HOOVER. And you don't care enough about her to want her to meet someone and be happy?

ANNE. You think she's going to be happy with him? If he ever calls her after tonight. Big if. And if they go out a few times and can stand each other, and even if they get married and have beautiful fucking kids, he will never make her happy.

HOOVER. Why not?

ANNE. Because she'll always be thinking that she could have done better. Found someone more interesting, better looking, funnier. Taller. You don't understand. *(Looking at her.)* She used to do really well, guys liked her, people liked her, she was fun. And then somehow she just ... lost something. She doesn't have the same confidence or self-respect, I don't know. You can see it, you know, look at her, she looks ready to be wounded.

HOOVER. That's called vulnerable.

ANNE. So? Vulnerable means you look like you're about to get your ass kicked. Why is that good?

HOOVER. Why is that bad?

ANNE. It's not bad, it's just pathetic, I think. It's not a quality I'd want to advertise.

HOOVER. What do you want to advertise?

ANNE. I don't want to advertise anything.

HOOVER. If you had to describe how you'd like to be seen.

ANNE. I don't know. You tell me.

HOOVER. Like you've got your shit together.

ANNE. Uh huh. But I don't ....

HOOVER. I just think you're bored. Bored with your life, bored with yourself, bored with that guy on the phone. I think you feel like nothing different happens to you any more and everybody looks the same and nothing really matters to you or excites you like it used to.

ANNE. *(Lets this sink in for a second.)* Is that so? Well listen, it's been a pleasure listening to your bullshit stories about people you don't know and your bullshit pop psychology about people you've just met but I really have to get going.

(She starts to get up.)

HOOVER. They're not talking any more.

ANNE. What?

HOOVER. He's talking to some other girl now. She went into the bathroom.

ANNE. Great. He made her real fuckin' happy.

HOOVER. *(He looks at her and shakes his head.)* That's cold.

ANNE. What? What does that mean? What the fuck do you know? She's my friend, it's my shoulder she's going to be crying on, I'm the one who'll listen to her and tell her it's gonna be okay, that he wasn't worth it anyway.

HOOVER. I didn't say that.

ANNE. *(Getting upset.)* What then? What? Do I have problems? Yes. Do I sometimes take them out on other people and be a bitch on the phone? Maybe. What the fuck business is it of yours? You don't know me, you don't know my friends.

HOOVER. I didn't say any of that.

ANNE. *(Almost shouting.)* So what, then. What are you saying?

HOOVER. *(A little rattled.)* Nothing. I'm not saying anything. *(Pause.)* Listen, do you, do you want a beer?

ANNE. What?

HOOVER. Beer. Do you want a beer?

ANNE. *(Calming down.)* Uh, no. No thanks. *(He gets a cooler out from under the table in front of him, opens a beer for himself.)* What's that?

HOOVER. My cooler.

ANNE. Yeah, I can see it's your cooler, why do you have a cooler? Why a cooler? You're at a party. It's not a picnic, there's a refrigerator here.

HOOVER. *(Shaking his head, he's been down that road before.)* Uh huh, that's not for me. The fridge at a party? No way. Doesn't work, someone always gets screwed. I'm happy to b my own b, but it's gonna stay my own b, you know?

ANNE. But you offered me a b.

HOOVER. Hey, I'll give away all my b, I'm not stingy, but if I give it away, I want to know where it's going, you know? I don't know these people, I don't want them in my stuff.

ANNE. You said you'd introduce me around, you must know somebody.

HOOVER. Nope.

ANNE. Well who'd you come with?

HOOVER. No one. I live down the street, I heard some people

talking about a party and thought I'd check it out.

ANNE. So you know no one here.

HOOVER. No one.

ANNE. *(Beat.)* So you're basically trespassing?

HOOVER. I wouldn't call it that.

ANNE. What would you call it?

HOOVER. I don't know, hanging out.

ANNE. No, it's not even hanging out. It's hovering. You're undermining the whole purpose of the party. You're the anti-party. You're like a one-man wrecking crew. I mean parties are supposed to be social events, right? Well what do you do exactly? You sit here by yourself, completely isolated, *(She picks up his cooler.)* protecting your cooler of beer—

HOOVER. *(Interrupts.)* I offered you a beer.

ANNE. —You make up stories in your head about these people you don't know, and you eavesdrop on people's conversations. *(Beat. She rests her case.)* Am I right?

HOOVER. I don't know. Basically.

(She opens a beer and sits back on the couch considering this, trying it for herself. She nods her head and looks at him, then back at the party.)

ANNE. I could see that.

(She takes a swig. He smiles. Blackout.)

END OF THE PLAY

Jerry Springer Is God

MATT PELFREY

Jerry Springer Is God

by
Matt Pelfrey

*premiered in January, 2001 at
Actors Theatre of Louisville*

Directed by Sullivan Canaday White
Dramaturg: Tanya Palmer

Cast

Viv	Star Xavier Little
Laura	Emera Felice Krauss
Dana	Lia Aprile
RC	Peter Stone
Jim	Alex Finch
Tex	Nehal Joshi

Scenic Designer: Brenda Ellis
Costume Designer: Karen Hall
Lighting Designer: Andrew Vance
Sound Designer: Kate Ducey
Properties Designer: Dan Tracy
Stage Manager: Erin Tatge
Assistant Stage Manager: Sarah Hodges
Fight Director: Brent Langdon

CHARACTERS

TEX: male, late teens, early 20's
RC: male, late teens. early 20's
JIM: male, late teens, early 20's
VIV: female, late teens, early 20's
LAURA: female, late teens, early 20's
DANA: female, late teens, early 20's

TIME AND PLACE

Near the end of the 20th Century. An apartment.

Jerry Springer Is God

(A funky living room.
Five unmatched chairs are in the center of the room. Sitting in these
chairs are VIV, LAURA, DANA, RC and JIM. TEX stands off to
the side watching them.)

VIV. She's been sleeping with my man!

LAURA. I have not!

VIV. Oh yes you have!

LAURA. I don't know what this bitch is trippin' about!

VIV. Bullshit! I see how you check him out! You call my place
when you know *damn well* I'm at work!

LAURA. Oh, stop your lying! And don't *even* pretend that's your
real hair!

VIV. Excuse me?

LAURA. Did I stutter? You're bald, ass-ugly and there is no way
in hell I would go sniffing around some piece of trailer park tube-
steak like him!

(VIV gets up and rushes at LAURA. LAURA meets her half way and
they start to struggle with each other. Their fight is rather pa-
thetic. After a minute of this they both start to laugh and turn to
TEX.)

VIV. This is *so* stupid.

LAURA. It really is.

TEX. No, come on! You're doing great!

RC. Nice try, but this is not gonna work.

TEX. You guys, don't do this to me....

JIM. We've humored you long enough. Slap that video in. Move
these chairs back.

TEX. Come on! Hold up....

JIM. Who wants more grog?

VIV. Right here. Grab me an Anchor Steam.

LAURA. *(Raising her hand.)* Rolling Rock.

RC. See, Tex, we can't go on that show for one basic reason; we aren't freaks. We aren't mutants. We are normal. We're real. We have all our teeth. We aren't humping our brothers and sisters and living in trailers.

LAURA. He's right, Tex. Everyone they parade on that show is a cockroach.

VIV. ... Trailer park monstrosities.

DANA. One guy was so inbred, I could swear I saw *gills* on him.

JIM. Iggy the Porpoise Boy.

TEX. So you do admit watching?

JIM. Of course. Human cockfighting is quality television.

RC. I think they should expand the premise of the show ... make it life or death ... like gladiator combat, search through all these small towns for human oddities and make them fight each other. Like they do with pit bulls. Not only would it clean out the gene pool but it gives us another spectator sport.

DANA. What a little Nazi you are.

JIM. That would be *humongous* entertainment. I would *pay* to see that.

DANA. Coming from a guy who's paid to see an armless stripper, that is not saying much.

JIM. First off, that was in Mexico. Second, I've always supported the rights of the handicapped, and third, she was a skilled dancer. It was an intensely erotic experience that I shall cherish into ripe old age. I swear, how many times are you going to bring that up?

RC. Why would we want to go on national television and humiliate ourselves while a studio full of sociopaths chant "Jerry! Jerry! Jerry!"

TEX. It's about the quest for interesting, human experiences. It's about taking off all your clothes and doing a big cannon ball dive into the cultural zeitgeist.

VIV. More like diving into the cultural sewage of late 20th Century television.

TEX. We cannot pass this up. I've got it all set. I've got one of the producers hooked and I'm ready to reel the bastard in. He just wants to meet with the rest of you, conduct a pre-show interview ...

we are *in there*.

VIV. You mean this guy is already interested in us?

TEX. After the shit I slung at him, bet your ass he is.

LAURA. I'm confused ... what in the hell would we go on the show and say?

TEX. That's what I was hoping we could hash-out tonight. That's what our little improv was about...

JIM. So your concept is we lie? That's your plan?

TEX. I prefer to think of it as role-playing, but basically, yeah. We'll lie our asses off.

LAURA. This is so inane.

JIM. Really Tex, no offense, I want you to feel like you can come to us with anything. I think as friends it's important to be a sanctuary where you can be comfortable sharing any idea, thought or feeling ... but this is one of the most utterly stupid ideas I have ever wasted my time listening to, and if you ever try to foist another idea this pathetic on us again, I'll stand on a chair and pee on you.

TEX. You guys have no vision. Like it or not, "Springer" is a trademark of our times. And think about it ... wouldn't it be cool to be able to say we were a part of it? The boomers had their marches and protests....

VIV. Did you know three out of five claim they were at Woodstock—

DANA. A mathematical impossibility.

TEX. Right, but listen ... "Springer" is not long for this world. Powerful forces are already surrounding him ... pressuring him to clean up his act, to sanitize his wacky hijinks. But mark my words: the "Springer" show is going to go down in TV history as a legend. Twenty years from now, some Oliver Stone wannabe is going to make a three hour biopic of this cat's life ... and we'll be able to say we were on the show. It's gonna be a *classic*. Think of it like being on "American Bandstand," except with bitch-slapping, hair-pulling and an occasional thrown shoe.

RC. I have to disagree with Jimbo. I think Tex is making a provocative, compelling case.

LAURA. The hell he is. They're already touchy about those fake fight accusations. We can't pull this off even if we all agreed to your little scheme.

TEX. You don't think you're smart enough to fool the producers of "The Jerry Springer" show? Is that what you're saying? *(Beat.)* We could totally pull this off! It'll be epic!

JIM. So what would our yarn be?

TEX. Well, this is just what I've kinda thrown together ... feel free to mix and match, but okay, here it is: Viv will go on and say she wants to confront her boyfriend with a dark secret, okay? I'll come in and she'll tell me she's having an affair with Jim. Jim will come in, I'll charge Jim and we'll choreograph a little fight. Then Jim will say he's got a secret of his own. And he'll say he's been sleeping with Dana, who will say she was supposed to be Viv's maid of honor at her upcoming wedding. Then RC, you come in and rush Jim, saying you're Dana's boyfriend.

JIM. That's a crappy scenario.

TEX. Well, come up with something else ... it's not written in *stone*.

DANA. I'm not doing it.

JIM. Me neither.

LAURA. Good. That's settled. Let's watch a video. What is it we rented?

VIV. "Bring me the Head of Alfredo Garcia." Peckenpah.

TEX. You guys suck. I can't believe you won't rise to the occasion.

RC. I dunno ... it almost sounds fun, except I think you'd need to work on the scenario a little more.

TEX. Let's hear your critique.

RC. Well, you've kinda got a credibility problem....

TEX. Where?

RC. The Jim-Dana thing.

TEX. Yeah, so?

RC. It's just not ... credible.

TEX. Why not?

RC. C'mon ... I mean ... "come on." *(Looks around.)* Someone help me out here.

JIM. No. What exactly do you mean?

RC. *(Thinks a moment, trying to be as diplomatic as he can.)* I just think if the plan is to go on national television and perform what is basically a hoax, we should have a plot that lends itself to the suspension of disbelief a *tad more*.

JIM. What's not believable about me and Dana having an affair?

RC. Isn't it obvious?

JIM. No, it's not. Educate me.

DANA. Let's not and say we did. Throw in the video.

JIM. I want to know what he fucking means.

RC. *(He looks at JIM for a beat or two before speaking.)* Who's gonna believe you could get somewhere with Dana? I mean, I'm sorry, but the issue had to be brought up.

DANA. Ray, why do you always have to do shit like this?

RC. Like what? If we're gonna go on this show we have to—

DANA. *(Frustrated, angry.)* We're not going on the goddamn show! Let's just drop this and have a nice little time watching this movie!

TEX. Ray, what are you trying to do here, man—

RC. You can't go on the tube with *science fiction*, okay? We have to be able to suspend disbelief or—

JIM. You don't think I could ....

LAURA. Time out! Time fucking out!

JIM. Wait—

LAURA. No! We are forgetting this crap right now! I'm not going to have you guys in here talking about who could score with who, like we're just ... appliances or something, not even in the room!! Fuck that!

JIM. *(Ignoring LAURA.)* Hold on! I don't have a shot with Dana? Is that your statement?

RC. *(Mockingly pretends to think it over.)* Um ... yep.

JIM. And why is that?

TEX. We're getting off track here. None of this is serious, okay? Jim ... Jimbo ... you're a studley, sexual predator ... any woman would gratefully accept your manhood in a heartbeat. Okay? Are egos healed now? Can we move on?

JIM. Tex?

TEX. Yo?

JIM. Shut up and sit down. *(To RC.)* Why couldn't I get anywhere with someone like Dana?

DANA. Ladies, are we gonna let shit go on? Viv? You've been quiet over there ....

VIV. I'd kinda like to know RC's answer.

DANA. This is *so* stupid.

RC. You wanna know?

TEX. No, she doesn't, let's—

RC. There are leagues in everything. Take baseball. You've got pee-wee league. Little league. High school. The professional minors and of course, major league baseball. You follow so far?

TEX. Just get to the point so we can move past this, please....

DANA. I'm outta here!

(DANA exits down a hallway.)

TEX. You guys are really fucking up my plans. I could get some tasty exposure being on that show and—

JIM. *(To RC.)* I said, go on.

RC. Think of Dana, then look in the mirror. She's the majors, so to speak, and you, this pains me to say, are still running around in the pee-wee league.

JIM. *(To the others.)* Can you guys believe this?

LAURA. Ray, you are being so goddamn stupid its not even funny.

RC. I'm just giving it to you straight.

TEX. I hate to break the news to you, RC, but I've seen Alec Baldwin on the movie screen, I've seen him on television, and you sir, are no Alec Baldwin.

RC. What the fuck are you talking about?

JIM. I guess you don't talk to Dana much.

RC. What's that supposed to mean?

JIM. I mean, there's not a lot of sharing between the two of you. Maybe you should spend some time talking. You might learn something.

RC. Like what? What should I be learning about my girlfriend? Educate me.

TEX. Alright, fuck this. Fuck Jerry Springer. You guys are—

VIV. What's up with Dana?

JIM. Viv, shut up.

TEX. Hey, hey, hey—

VIV. I'm on your side here—

JIM. I don't need help with—

RC. Wait, wait, wait ... what is this?

TEX. I'm getting some brews.

(DANA enters wearing her jacket. She heads for the front door.)

RC. Whoa, where are you going—?

DANA. Home.

RC. Come here....

DANA. Fuck off.

RC. What the hell is this? Get over here!

JIM. Easy....

RC. Fuck you. *(Shoves JIM.)* Say what you have to say! You got advice for me punk? *(Shoves him again.)* Say it!

JIM. *(Shoves RC away.)* Forget it....

RC. *(Moves close to JIM.)* Say it! *(Shoves JIM.)* Spill your guts! *(Shoves JIM.)* Tell me! What is behind that shit eating grin you're always wearing?

DANA. Stop it, Ray!

(RC tries to shove JIM again. JIM grabs RC's arms, looks him in the eyes.)

JIM. You want me to spill my guts? That what you want Mr. Major League?

RC. Yeah, that's what I want....

JIM. Then take one guess who's been groovin' on my stick....

TEX. Aw, crap....

RC. *(To DANA.)* You slept with him?

JIM. Fucking is really a more appropriate word there, Ray. Looks like I just took a step up to the majors—

(RC dives on JIM. They go sprawling into the couch, fighting each other.)

LAURA. *(Looking over at DANA, her voice quivering with rage.)* The two of you...?

DANA. I can explain—

LAURA. YOU FUCKING BITCH!!

(LAURA takes off her shoe and throws it at DANA, missing. LAURA charges DANA, they start fighting. TEX and VIV try to pull the different combatants apart but are themselves pulled into the insane tangle of punches, bites, kicking, and hair pulling.

As the chaos continues, the sound of "The Jerry Springer Show" rises. A TV audience chants "Jerry! Jerry! Jerry!" over and over as lights fade.)

END OF THE PLAY

Fiddle and Faddle

TOM GLIATTO

Fiddle and Faddle

by
Tom Gliatto

*premiered in August, 2002 at
Actors Theatre of Louisville*

Directed by Sullivan Canaday White
Dramaturg: Elizabeth Nolte

Cast

Fiddle	Timothy Tamisiea
Faddle	Johnny Lin

Lighting Designer: Matt Gard
Costume Designer: John White
Sound Designer: Matt Hubbs
Properties Designer: Ann Marie Werner
Stage Manager: Sue Semaan

Fiddle and Faddle

(A pool in the White House. Three deck chairs.
FIDDLE and FADDLE: Both very pretty, early 20s, in bikinis and
hairstyles suitable to the 1960s. One should be blond, the other a
redhead. FIDDLE, maybe, should be the latter.
A small metal table with perhaps martinis and an ashtray. The sound
of water lapping in the pool.
FADDLE is smoking. Stubs out the cigarette almost angrily, then
picks up a fashion magazine and thumbs through it impatiently,
noisily. FIDDLE naps in a deck chair.
FIDDLE's delivery is perhaps softer than FADDLE's, with a touch of
Marilyn Monroe.
FIDDLE wakes up with a start.)

FADDLE. You fell asleep, Miss Fiddle.

FIDDLE. Did I? Well, yes obviously I did. Sorry. I was feeling a
little—and then I was having these dreams—

FADDLE. It would have been disappointing if he came down
here in his trunks and bathrobe, all ready to have a go at it, you know,
really ready to have a go, and there you are snoring. Not that you
snored. But if you allow yourself a deep enough nap you may. And
then the acoustic tiles amplify everything. When Louis XV caught
Madame Pompadour napping, he banished her to Bavaria.

(FIDDLE looks at her watch.)

FIDDLE. Seven o'clock already. Faddle, maybe he won't be
coming tonight....

FADDLE. *(Sitting.)* Well I think it may be a little hard for him,
leader of the free world at the center of the spinning wheel of history,
to pull himself out of those meetings. I could hear the doors in the

great corridors of power slam shut all the way down here. And the bolts! I doubt he'll have time to comb his thick flaxen hair, poor man. On the other hand the stress is probably tremendous, and he might at some point desire to pay us a visit. And then we will, you know, frolic as usual. So please do be frolicsome, hm? You have had a disconcerting floaty quality all day. I would almost think you would not welcome a visit from our President.

FIDDLE. No no. But I wonder do we seem—superfluous—at a time like this, assuming it does amount to a world crisis. The big men at the helm of the ship, the ladies below, forgotten among the mangoes and salt cod and camels and so forth, and the screaming children ....

FADDLE.. I am not superfluous. We are not superfluous. They also serve who—serve. We are, in our way, essential, or he would not have us here round the clock on red alert, so to speak, next to naked. Yes. And just remember this if you ever doubt your importance: You are giving the best years of your life to your country and to your President. Even if you do nothing but wait by the pool until he comes ambling in and throws us into the water and rips off our tops and has sex with us. *(Looking at her magazine again, but not relaxing.)* I am not ashamed to say I regard myself as a patriot. *(Puts the magazine down.)* And I will tell you—the greatest betrayal either of us could commit? If, by some preposterous and cruel turn of events, Castro were to take over the country, and he drove into Washington in his jeep and dusty beard and he were to say, "Fiddle and Faddle? This is Fidel! I am coming down to the pool to taste the succulent fruits that so delighted the President"—well, I would drown myself before he even removed his filthy underwear. And I would take you with me with my arms draped around your neck like heavy seaweed. No I will never ever sleep with a communist. Not even doze. Sleep with the President, and the President only, and be a patriot. Sleep with a communist and be a whore. "Punta" I think is the word. I mean, you can imagine the sort of girls he, Castro, keeps on hand to— Well, yes, as I said, puntas. Vicious girls from the country sleeping their way up the party ranks. Filthy little opportunists, which is a far cry from patriot. And, revolution being what it is, you can bet those girls will end up on the dustbin of history. Broken like the little pathetic dolls they are! There is no fidelity in Fidel. Ha! Whereas you and I, F and F, have been treated to night education classes at Vassar by the Secret Service, and finishing classes with the same woman who trained the first lady, and the President's doctor treats us routinely for the infections that are a regrettable consequence of the job. I think we could "pass," so to speak, in Hyannisport. Except that we're not allowed there, no of course not. Our place is here by the pool, expecting and then pleasuring the President. Imagine how the family would feel, after all, they're out playing touch football or sailing or some typical Irish Catholic activity, and who should stroll by but Fiddle and Faddle in their bikinis? Duty! Duty! Duty!

FIDDLE. Are you all right, Faddle?

FADDLE. Of course I am.

FIDDLE. Well—how grave is it, this crisis, do you think?

FADDLE. Well, Fiddle, as we are not on the National Security Council or in the cabinet, that would be hard to say, wouldn't it? We are not pretty little flies on the alabaster walls of state. We are poolside in our bikinis in the White House basement.

FIDDLE. But wouldn't it be awful if everyone blew up? Our bodies in the same instant liquefied by the heat, and then baked into cinder.... Like a crematorium, only on an uncommonly apocalyptic scale.... The children ....

FADDLE. That is not really your concern. Is it? Besides, this is about preserving our way of life. *Way* of life. Not the same *as* life. I mean democracy and so forth. I would rather have all the children in this nation—and pets, for that matter—dead and free in heaven than bent under the yoke of Castro, or Khruschev, or any of their like. Remember that, even as you blow up!

FIDDLE. Faddle, I think you *are* being a little—something.

FADDLE. Am I?

FIDDLE. Strident? Overwrought?

FADDLE. If I am, it is only because you are becoming maudlin and sentimental over humanity, which is unpatriotic at this time. I mean, no offense, you could be shot for talking maudlin trash. And we are in the right morally, anyway, and that fact will not change even after the entire planet is dead and there is not one living life form left in all of the universe, not even some microscopic blob in a meteor. And as to death, so what? Big deal. There is the wise consul of Marcus Aurelius, who thank God I read in the original Latin at Vassar. In death, he said, one loses only a single moment, the present. The past is already behind, you see, and so does not exist. The future has not come to be, so *that* does not exist. Death is merely a moment. For a child, a moment. For a poodle, a moment. For a leaf, a moment. You lose that single moment of the present. See?

FIDDLE. *(Not really reassured.)* Thank you, Faddle.

FADDLE. Certainly. I told you to take Latin.

(Pause. FADDLE sits back.)

FIDDLE. Faddle, all my talk about children— *(Pause.)* I think I may be pregnant.

(FADDLE sits up.)

FADDLE. By whom?

FIDDLE. Well, by the President, I think. There is no other. Last I heard the boy I loved in high school was still being held by the Vietcong.

FADDLE. Are you sure?

FIDDLE. Yes of course. We are pledged to the President.

FADDLE. You know you have to get rid of it.

FIDDLE. Yes, I did assume that....

FADDLE. Because I got rid of mine.

FIDDLE. Oh. You never said.

FADDLE. No. I never did say. What's *to* say? Even if God shook me awake and told me I was carrying his only son, I would not keep that baby if it interfered with pleasuring my President. Jesus out with the bathwater! But you must get rid of it. The President likes us a twosome, and if you are so selfish as to have his child then you will completely throw off our sexual equilibrium and, for all I know, destabilize the President and throw the country and the world into utter gusting chaos—worse, I should think, than even nuclear war.

FIDDLE. Well, I will get rid of it. As soon as there is no nuclear holocaust.

FADDLE. Yes. Good, pragmatic planning. Good.

FIDDLE. Oh—does that imply you think there *won't* be war?

FADDLE. No. I did not say that. I don't know, Fiddle.

FIDDLE. It's just—the thing that I find strange is.... I have been sitting here thinking about nuclear weapons, and nuclear war, and all the children in the world being destroyed, reduced to cinders and curling up into a flaming sky. That was what I dreamed, that. All the cinders floating up, the way the air will stir them and suck them up in the fireplace and up out the chimney and into the night. Only they were babies. Little orange glowing fetuses. And I think of this one never getting a chance to see anything of life. There will be no world for it. And as a result I feel—a sadness that I have never .... —Think, Faddle, no world. No—circuses or Christmas wrapping or apple turnovers —I mean, those are simply happy associations of mine, they mean nothing in the larger scheme. Except that I associate them, too, with my mother, who was so good to me, to everyone. *(She is getting tearful, then.)* And I suspect would have had a significantly different take on patriotic duty than yours. Yet I will get rid of it, I will, the baby. In which case it will know nothing of anything, regardless. *(Sighs.)* I don't know. This *does* seem such a sad—conundrum? Or maybe not. I mean, you know—perhaps when the crisis is ended, and I am finished with the White House—I assume the President will tire of me while I am still somewhere in my reproductive years—maybe there will be *other* children I can have, only by some nonpolitical figure, an engineer or a businessman or minister and—oh, it just makes me *sad,* what can I say? *(Crying a little.)* Inexpressibly sad. And is it, is this sadness, is it new to me because nuclear war is new? Or because pregnancy is new? I can't parse out my feelings....

FADDLE.. I got rid of mine immediately. Sooner the better. The President will not want—

FIDDLE. *(Losing her temper.)* Oh, Faddle, please shut up! Women, even mistresses, are *meant* to give life. Simple biology! Communist women too! Aren't there seven or six little Khruschevs? *I* was meant to give life. And here I am by a pool waiting for the President or waiting for death, and my poor mother died thinking I would probably settle down with Jeff, except for the Viet Cong, and that's assuming he actually didn't defect—and the Secret Service has given me this stupid name—and—and—I *am* superfluous, Faddle, I have been rendered superfluous. And I am not supposed to be! You know what? It's *women* who bring life into the world, and men who bring death. I am vital to the world, not the President. And also! Also— how can death be just a moment, as Marcus Aurelius says, or you say, or whoever, if everything is totally dead in the universe for all time? That is not a moment. That is eternity. I know the difference between eternity and a moment!

(FADDLE gets up and grips her.)

FADDLE. Now, look. I am trying to let you talk yourself out, but obviously you will keep talking even if there is a nuclear holocaust. Everything is fine! All right? Look. All right.

FIDDLE. Yes, but it is not all right.

FADDLE. Everything—!

FIDDLE. Nothing! Faddle, I can see it in your eyes. All day I've seen it in your eyes.

FADDLE. Fiddle, I explained to you that principle—democracy, the Four Freedoms, better dead than red, fry the Rosenbergs—overrides everything here! Even if the President were never to come down here again, if he were to be buried under radioactive debris and—Oh, Jesus. Oh. *(She collapses onto her chair.)* The President *must* come. If this is the end, if I die without seeing him this last time —! Oh my God I love him so much. And yet he can never keep straight who's Fiddle, who's Faddle. And I have to share him, oh the humiliation of it! You and his wife and Marilyn Monroe.

FIDDLE. Marilyn? Is that true?

FADDLE. Yes of course it is! I want her dead so much! But you —the sharing with *you,* that's the worst of it. What can I do but bear it? I can't tell the President how to love me! But to die here without him! Isn't it so—don't you love him too? Can it be possible any woman does *not* love him? Don't you hate sharing him with me? Although if you in fact do—do in fact love him—that makes you a rival, and if say we came down to being the last three people on earth, I would allow him to have a couple of children by you, which I gather would satisfy you, fine, and then I would *kill* you. With a glowing red-hot brick or whatever comes to hand. Then I would let him screw me and give him all the children he wanted. And of course given the family, Irish Catholics, I would essentially be a post-nuclear rabbit. I would repopulate the world within two generations. Great guns. But I assure you, Fiddle, and I warn you, I would kill for love. Of him. And that is not patriotism I am talking about now. That is love. Pure love.

(FADDLE breaks down. FIDDLE pats her shoulder.)

FIDDLE. I've never loved the President that way, Faddle. I think I would prefer his brother, actually. He seems more delicate. Less inclined to make me strip on the diving board and then dive even though I can only cannonball.

FADDLE. *(A bit more cheerful.)* Well, I will take what grim consolation I can from that, Faddle. Thank you. Well!

(Pause.)

> FIDDLE. You see? It *is* stressful. The missiles.
> FADDLE. And love.
> FIDDLE. Children. Life. Death. Yes....

(Pause. The sound of footsteps echoing. FIDDLE looks over.)

> FADDLE. Is it?
> FIDDLE. Yes. Oh this is embarrassing.
> FADDLE. No. Duty. It is our duty. We are patriots.
> FIDDLE. Yes. Okay.
> FADDLE. Ready?
> FIDDLE. Yes.

(They turn and girlishly cry out, cooing sympathetically, and hold out their arms.)

> FIDDLE and FADDLE. Mr. President!

END OF THE PLAY

Trash Anthem

DAN DIETZ

Trash Anthem

by
Dan Dietz

premiered in April, 2003 at the
Humana Festival of New American Plays

Directed by Jennifer Hubbard
Dramaturg: Steve Moulds

Cast

Woman	Rebecca Wisocky
Boots	Michael Laurence

Scenic Designer: Paul Owen
Costume Designers: John P. White and Mike Floyd
Lighting Designer: Paul Werner
Sound Designer: Colbert S. Davis IV
Properties Designer: Doc Manning
Stage Manager: Leslie K. Oberhausen
Assistant Stage Managers: Michael Domue and Andrew Scheer

Trash Anthem

(Little house. Big South. A pair of men's cowboy BOOTS. WOMAN stands in cheap but professional clothing. She holds a shovel. Her body is streaked with dirt. She stomps the shovel to the floor three times, then turns to the BOOTS and approaches them in a slow march, stomping a rhythm with the shovel.)

WOMAN. *(Sings under her breath:)*
    I am earthy
    I am raw
    My man's in pieces
    Down in the soggy soggy

(She stands next to the BOOTS in silence. Drops the shovel. Raises her hands above her head, screams, and thrusts her hands into the BOOTS. WOMAN pulls out her hands—they are covered in rich black soil. She's got fistfuls of it.)

*   *   *   *   *   *

(New start. A pair of men's cowboy BOOTS. WOMAN slowly approaches them. She stops, considers them for a moment, then shifts the BOOTS so the left boot is on the right side and the right boot on the left. She smiles to herself, walks off. Pause. The BOOTS talk to the audience.)

BOOTS. Ow. Goddammit. Hey. 'Scuse me. Y'all in the seats there. Yeah, could one of you, uh, come down here and move these back? Please? I'm serious, this hurts. Come on. One of you men take pity one. I'm twisted up genital-wise. Please?

*   *   *   *   *   *

(New start. WOMAN stands by BOOTS.)

WOMAN. My man ain't a cowboy. 'Cept at his feet. Cowboy feet, leather-wrapped and stinky. My man ain't a cowboy.

My man ain't a talker. 'Cept with his hands. Talking hands, reach out and touch someone, long distance cellular kinda hands, still feel 'em back of my neck, gripping in a man way, slipping in that same man way, you know, down. Ain't a talker, nope.

So I fell in love with his hands and his feet. We'd go dancing, and I'd spend the whole time looking down at his boots. Felt like as long as I kept my eyes locked on them, we could dance across the Gulf of Mexico and never fall in. I loved them hard, those feet, those hands. Listened hard to the heartbeats at the tips of his fingers and toes. Tried to decipher. Unravel the code in blood flow. Find the secret that binds forever.

Failed.

(WOMAN raises her hands, screams, thrusts them into the BOOTS, pulls out fistfuls of earth. The BOOTS scream back. The WOMAN smiles.)

BOOTS. What do you want from me?

WOMAN. Talk.

BOOTS. I don't talk, you know that.

WOMAN. I know. You use your hands. Crack open peanuts when I'm talking to you. Stare at the wall.

BOOTS. I communicate through peanuts, like all men do. I pop the little buggers out of their shells like mussels, like mollusks, like deep-sea snails. I dip them behind my lips, shake the half-shell, rattle 'em into my mouth. And then I crunch. And this combination of pop, rattle, crunch is a language. Sweeter'n English.

WOMAN. You ain't gonna be popping peanuts no more.

BOOTS. Nope. Got myself popped instead.

WOMAN. Your own fault.

BOOTS. Hardly deserving of an execution.

WOMAN. I was pissed off.

BOOTS. Oh. Well. In that case fire away.

WOMAN. I did! *(Pause.)* I hope it didn't hurt.

BOOTS. Course it hurt! Jesus.

WOMAN. Sorry.

BOOTS. Me too.

WOMAN. But you deserved it.

Wish to god this story was more original, folks, but it ain't. I swore when I started paralegal classes I wasn't gonna live the stereotype no more. But here I am, stuck back in that same old same old white trash anthem: Woman finds her man with his dick inside the neighbor. Woman grabs the rifle off the rack. Blah-de-blah-de-blah. It ain't fair. I drive a Jetta.

BOOTS. Well, there is a twist.

WOMAN. Ain't no twist.

BOOTS. Oh, there's a twist all right.

WOMAN. Shut up.

BOOTS. See, folks, what Genevieve ain't saying ....

WOMAN. Don't you say another word!

BOOTS. What Genevieve ain't exactly being forthcoming about is the fact that ....

WOMAN. I said, shut it! *(She grips the BOOTS at the top, squeezes them shut. The BOOTS continue talking, muffled and incomprehensible. She sings:)*

> I am earthy
> I am raw
> My man's in pieces
> Down in the soggy soggy

(BOOTS are silent.) Hey. You gonna behave? *(No answer.)* You ain't gonna make me regret this are you? *(No answer.)* Okay.

(WOMAN releases BOOTS.)

BOOTS. The neighbor was a man.

WOMAN. GODDAMMIT!

BOOTS. Sorry, babe, they got a right to know. It was a man, folks. The dick she is referring to was deep inside a—

WOMAN. PLEASE! Shit.

BOOTS. Jesus, you can be so Stone Age. Twenty-first century, Jenny. Wake up and smell the tolerance.

WOMAN. I just don't get it. You were so butch.

(Pause.)

BOOTS. Did you get Jeff, too?

WOMAN. Nope. He's fast.

BOOTS. More ways'n one.

WOMAN. You mighta got away too, if you hadn't had your boots on. Stuck in the sheets like a drowning man. Boots in bed. Walking on water.

BOOTS. He's got the police headed your way right now.

WOMAN. Probably. How long you been like this?

BOOTS. I don't know. How old are my veins?

WOMAN. I loved you. I gave you a home. We danced. You ever dance with Jeff?

BOOTS. In this town? We'd get our asses kicked.

WOMAN. I'd pay money to see that.

BOOTS. Look. You shot me, okay? You buried me in the back-yard, you win. What more do you want?

WOMAN. I don't know.

BOOTS. Well then, woman, LET ME IN PEACE.

(WOMAN screams at BOOTS. BOOTS scream back. Silence.)

WOMAN. How many?

BOOTS. Besides Jeff?

WOMAN. How many *times. (Pause.)* I never cheated on you.

BOOTS. Okay. Thanks.

WOMAN. *(Stomps the toe of a boot.)* FUCK YOU.

BOOTS. Ow. Goddamn, Jenny, these are my dancing boots. *(Pause.)* You gonna turn yourself in?

WOMAN. Nope.

BOOTS. They're gonna find out.

WOMAN. Maybe.

BOOTS. No maybe about it. You're going down. They're gonna slice your eyes open with them flashing blue lights. Till you tell 'em all your secrets.

WOMAN. Wish I could work that kinda magic on you. Man flows to your doorstep. You let him in. Man flows over the house, his smell washes everything in your home, a weird kinda clean. Saltwater clean. Let him in. Makes life a mystery. Confusion. The bed a place of foreign noises. Muffled sounds. And you can't for the life of you get the water outta your ears.

BOOTS. I didn't mean to get everything in a snarl.

WOMAN. Two years, you and me. When was Jeff?

BOOTS. June. Four months.

WOMAN. He's got a sunken chest.

BOOTS. Nothing makes sense, you know that.

WOMAN. More peanut talk.

(Sirens in the distance, getting closer.)

BOOTS. They're coming.

WOMAN. Yep. Listen. I turned my pockets inside out for you. I turned my self inside out. Can't you give me something? Something real, something I can hold in my hands for just a second?

BOOTS. Like what?

WOMAN. When you said you loved me, what did that mean?

BOOTS. There's a mole on your back, the one shaped like the Statue of Liberty.

WOMAN. Bullshit.

BOOTS. Well, like the torch part anyway. I loved that mole.

WOMAN. Not good enough.

(Sirens getting closer.)

BOOTS. There was a way you dug your fingers into me when we made love. Like you were gonna leave your prints on my bones. Like some kinda fossil.

WOMAN. You loved that?

BOOTS. Scared me.

WOMAN. Not good enough.

BOOTS. Baby, I used you, I'm sorry, you're here, I'm not, you're up on the ground and walking around, I'm dead and bleeding and sinking into the soggy soil right beneath your feet! NOW WHAT THE HELL I GOT YOU WANT?

(WOMAN screams. BOOTS scream. Sirens outside scream. WOMAN thrusts her hands into the BOOTS, still screaming. Suddenly, WOMAN and BOOTS aren't screaming—they're singing. As they sing, the WOMAN dances on all fours, her hands in the boots.)

BOOTS.	WOMAN.
Sea-water body	I am earthy

These boots can't hold me	I am raw
Salt-fingers touching to your lips	My man's in pieces
Still we danced	Down in the soggy soggy
Always you drink me	I am earthy
Always you thirsty	I am raw
Can't get the water past your lips	My man's in pieces
Still we danced	Still we danced

(Blue lights flow around the room. It looks like they're surrounded by an ocean of water. Sound of waves crashing. Then pounding on the door. The blue lights speed up—police lights. WOMAN rises, removes her hands from the BOOTS. She picks up the shovel. Pounding on the door. WOMAN stares defiantly out to the audience and stomps the shovel to the floor.
Blackout.)

END OF THE PLAY

Fit for Feet

JORDAN HARRISON

Fit for Feet

by
Jordan Harrison

*premiered in April, 2003 at the
Humana Festival of New American Plays*

Directed by Timothy Douglas
Dramaturg: Steve Moulds

Cast

Claire	Holli Hamilton
Linda	Celia Tackaberry
Jimmy	Greg McFadden
A Prominent Dance Critic	Shannon Holt

Scenic Designer: Paul Owen
Costume Designers: John P. White and Mike Floyd
Lighting Designer: Paul Werner
Sound Designer: Colbert S. Davis IV
Properties Designer: Doc Manning
Stage Manager: Leslie K. Oberhausen
Assistant Stage Managers: Michael Domue and Andrew Scheer

*This play is indebted to
Joan Acocella's unexpurgated edition of Nijinsky's diaries.*

CHARACTERS

CLAIRE: late twenties. Nice sweater set. Pastels.
LINDA: fifties. Improbably blonde for her age.
JIMMY: late twenties. Average Joe in a baseball cap.
A PROMINENT DANCE CRITIC: female.

Fit for Feet

Scene 1

*(Stage left. LINDA and CLAIRE in Adirondack chairs. LINDA re-
clines, sipping an iced tea. CLAIRE sits very straight, no iced
tea.)*

LINDA. Isn't this civilized?
CLAIRE. It is the ultimate goal of civilization to sit and do nothing.

(This silences LINDA for a second.)

LINDA. How are my almost-newlyweds? How are my daughter
and my wonderful new son?
CLAIRE. Jimmy thinks he's Nijinsky. The dancer. *(With added
difficulty.)* Recently he's started to believe he's Nijinsky.

*(Stage right. JIMMY is sawing the heels off a pair of dress shoes.
CLAIRE can see him but LINDA cannot.)*

LINDA. Does he dance?
CLAIRE. Not well, so you wouldn't think—
LINDA. I adore dancing.
CLAIRE. That really isn't the issue.
LINDA. The ballet in particular. Old World beauty. Strong male
legs. *Lifting.*
CLAIRE. Listen to me. I think he might be losing his mind. He
thinks he's a dead Russian.
LINDA. Might he be right?
CLAIRE. Jimmy has never been to Russia. He sits at a desk

every day. He is not a dancer.

LINDA. *(Airily.)* We should go to the ballet. *(CLAIRE gives her a look. Stage right, JIMMY is finished with his sawing. He tries the shoes on. Success: ballet slippers.)* You might take a look at the seating chart. For the reception. *(Pause. CLAIRE has noticed JIMMY putting on the "slippers.")* Mr. Barkley is at the same table as that Arkansas woman, and you know that won't do. *(CLAIRE gets out of her chair and crosses to JIMMY. He is doing pliés now, his back to her. Calling after her.)* You might consider!

(LINDA takes a resigned sip of iced tea. Her light fades.)

CLAIRE. Can I ask what you're doing?

(JIMMY stops cold, but doesn't turn around. We can see that there is music in his head.)

JIMMY. My head's full of strange names. Diaghilev, Stravinsky, Ballet Russes. Romola, Kyra, Kostrovsky. But above all, Diaghilev. How I hate that diseased dog, and love him. As I love all God's creations.

(He begins a different exercise.)

CLAIRE. Did anything happen recently, anything out of the ordinary?

(He turns to her.)

JIMMY. What is ordinary?
CLAIRE. Did you get hit on the head, did you cross a black cat, did you limbo a ladder?
JIMMY. There was the thing with the lightning.
CLAIRE. What with what?
JIMMY. I was walking along, minding my business—
CLAIRE. *(Gravely.)* That's how these things happen.
JIMMY. When out of the sky—
CLAIRE. Of course.
JIMMY. Would you mind not—
CLAIRE. Sorry.

JIMMY. Last Thursday. There hadn't been rain in the forecast, but I'm coming back from work—wouldn't you know, the sky is practically black. Jet black clouds, ions crashing in the air.

CLAIRE. Were you wearing your wedding shoes?

JIMMY. I figure I'll make it home in time if I take the shortcut through the field. *(CLAIRE's head is in her hands.)* On my way I see a cat up a tree, calico a few branches up. I start to climb, here kitty kitty, the storm all around me now. Then the kaboom.

CLAIRE. You didn't tell me this last Thursday.

JIMMY. *(A sudden, regal change, evidenced in his posture.)* Thursday, Friday. All is the same in the great wheel of life.

CLAIRE. Why Nijinsky? That's what I don't get. Why not Nureyev, Baryshnikov, one of the other Kovs?

JIMMY. *(Speaking of himself in the third person.)* Nijinsky is the best.

CLAIRE. You're not the best.

JIMMY. Wait and see.

(Stage left. Lights rise on LINDA.)

LINDA. You're hard on him, maybe that's it.

CLAIRE. I don't want there to be any illusions....

(CLAIRE returns to her chair.)

LINDA. Wait till you're married a year. Then you can turn shrew.

CLAIRE. ... Any secrets. It's destructive.

LINDA. Letting that lady minister do your vows—*that's* destructive.

CLAIRE. We can still call the whole thing off.

(LINDA removes a flask from her purse and pours something in her iced tea. She drinks deeply.)

LINDA. You left the iron on this morning.

CLAIRE. Oopsie.

LINDA. While you were dashing out.

CLAIRE. Good thing you saw it then.

(Stage right. JIMMY is drawing in a notebook with a crayon. Very

heavily—the crayon is soon down to a stub.)

LINDA. Exactly, good thing. Or what would have happened, Claire. You might take a moment to consider.

(CLAIRE doesn't take a moment.)

CLAIRE. The house would burn, the firemen would come, we arrive home to a charred black mess. You meet a kind fireman: big hands, a good cook. I hear those men are always good cooks. And I won't have to look after you ever again. Jimmy and I go live in some foreign, sun-dappled place. Help me find some oily rags, some lighter fluid. We'll do it right now!

LINDA. You haven't considered at all.

CLAIRE. I'm kind of preoccupied.

LINDA. Consider. Think of Muffin, for starters.

(Sound of a yippy dog yipping. They look off stage and back, quickly.)

CLAIRE. We would grieve.

LINDA. The photographs. Everything your memory has come to rely on, melted down to a bubbling chemical ooze-thing.

CLAIRE. A person can't live in the past.

LINDA. The CLOTHES, Claire. You have beautiful clothes.

CLAIRE. Insurance, Mother—

LINDA. —Can't replace the chenille scarf.

CLAIRE. Milan.

LINDA. That poncho doohickey.

CLAIRE. It's a *caftan*. Johannesburg.

LINDA. Earrings.

CLAIRE. Antique market, Copenhagen. *(With special pride.)* I haggled.

LINDA. Gorgeous.

CLAIRE. I thought so.

(JIMMY holds up his drawing, proudly, for the audience: many pairs of menacing eyes, peering out of darkness. CLAIRE sees it and recoils.)

LINDA. Have you considered? The absolute destruction of all

you've collected, all we've amassed that makes us us. All it takes is one everyday carelessness and POOF—what do you have, who ARE you now?

CLAIRE. I guess I hadn't considered.

(Blackout.)

Mini-Interlude

(JIMMY performs a demented little solo here between the two scenes. He begins very awkwardly, but grows in confidence, until there is a vigorous assurance to his movements. But he never ceases to be an average guy dancing ballet. Not Nijinsky.)

Scene 2

(CLAIRE and LINDA in the Adirondack chairs, as before. They are examining JIMMY's drawing.)

LINDA. Are those eyes?

CLAIRE. It's supposed to be soldiers, he told me.

LINDA. How creative.

CLAIRE. He's worse, I think. The other day I was all, "Darling, would you take a look at these china patterns?"

(JIMMY enters. He flings off his baseball cap, a romantic gesture— his hair smoothed off his forehead. Dapper. He acts out CLAIRE's narrative.)

CLAIRE. He walked up to me, looking me in the eye the whole time, grabbed my wrist, said:

JIMMY. I am noise. I am youth. I am a great hammer.

CLAIRE. Normally if a guy said that to me, *especially* my husband, I'd be: "Yeah sure, you're a hammer. Now about these patterns." But he looks at me that new way and says:

JIMMY. I am a rebel angel, Romola. You are a lusterless moon. You are fit for my feet.

CLAIRE. And he holds me and calls me by that strange name and I am *happy* to be fit for his feet.

LINDA. Susan Faludi wouldn't approve, Claire.

CLAIRE. *(In his grip.)* There's more. We're still in this violent, like, erotic, like, *clench* and he says:

JIMMY. I am God in my prick. God is in me and I am in God.

CLAIRE. *(Catching her breath.)* Say that again?

JIMMY. I am in God.

CLAIRE. No, the other.

JIMMY. I am God in my prick.

CLAIRE. *(Pouncing on him.)* That's the one.

LINDA. You must be delighted.

CLAIRE. Delighted? *(JIMMY crawls out from under CLAIRE and exits. She watches him leave.)* It's true, I can't help but find him somewhat more ... magnetic these days. This new confidence. Practicing jetés instead of scratching his pits.

LINDA. I'm not sure what you're complaining about.

CLAIRE. I don't *recognize* him. We're about to tell each other for better or for worse and I don't know who he is.

LINDA. Can we ever *know* a person, really? Why not be married to someone who wakes up different every morning? Every day a surprise.

CLAIRE. I chose *Jimmy*. That's what I want to wake up to. And maybe, every now and then, the virile and commanding Russian can come to visit.

LINDA. You were always the idealist, Claire.

CLAIRE. *(To herself.)* Maybe if I knew more about him.

LINDA. You've dated for it's been years.

CLAIRE. Nijinsky, I mean. If I did some research. Maybe this would make sense, if only we knew more.

(A prominent DANCE CRITIC enters. Haughty and urbane, she wears a dramatic, asymmetrical tunic. She reaches into the air and pulls down a white screen, center stage, without missing a beat. A slide of Nijinsky, in his famous Afternoon of a Faun *garb, appears.)*

CRITIC. Tragically, we lack a celluloid record of Nijinsky in performance.

But we know from first-hand accounts—among them, that of his great countryman Vladimir Nabokov—that when he leapt in the air, he seemed to hover for a moment, as if suspended by a gold thread leading out of his brow and through the roof.

Then, most remarkably, he lofted another inch before returning to Earth.

Every evening, audiences at the Ballets Russes witnessed an assault on the principles of gravity the like of which we haven't seen—unassisted by coarse machinery—since the Newtonian apple grounded mankind's Icarian fancies.

CLAIRE. What can she mean?

LINDA. Guy jumped high in the sky.

CRITIC. Next slide, please.

(The slide changes to Nijinsky, looking quite mad now, in Stravinsky's Petrushka.*)*

CRITIC. But if Nijinsky's leap embodied that part of us that wants to leave this world behind, it was his mind that finally carried out the dare.

CLAIRE. Pardon?

CRITIC. He went positively bonkers.

Abandoned by the ballet, the great man withdrew into the pages of his diary.

Written on three notebooks in 1919, the diary evidences a mind in which sex and war, heaven and hell simmer in the same debauched stew. A rondo of rigmarole, penned in an uneasy blend of his native Russian, courtly French, childlike scribblings, and a sort of malignantly repetitive baby-talk. Gobbledy-gook driven by a cunningly transgressive illogic. Mother Goose gone prick-mad. Muttering, proselytizing, scatologically obsessed, biting the heads off crayons, Nijinsky had become as much an animal as a God.

Is this the cost of genius? we ask the spheres.

We are still deciphering the music of their answer.

(The CRITIC curtsies deeply. Her light is extinguished. The screen flies away.)

LINDA. My head hurts.

CLAIRE. It will soon hurt more. Last night, he climbed out of bed, sleepwalking, he does that. *(JIMMY crosses, his arms stretched out, somnambulist-style.)* But never like this, all the way downstairs and out the front door. I put on a raincoat and followed him.

LINDA. A raincoat? With all your beautiful things...

CLAIRE. The most worrisome thing was he didn't trip once. Used to be he couldn't walk for his own shoelaces. Here he was, a bounce in his step—sidestepping cracks, sashaying past puddles, softly snoring all the time. Soon we're in a part of town I've never been to.

Cobblestones, steaming potholes. Can those be gaslights?

I can't even catch sight of a Starbucks.

He seems to be practicing steps: his arms striking the air, his legs like scissors.

As I watch him, I can almost hear the music he's dancing to,

and it's like he's lighter on his feet with every step.

People notice. All the motleys out at 3 AM:

Insomniacs with dark rings, child molesters, women with frosted hair. *(LINDA gasps.)*

They all come out of the shadows and follow him,

They don't know why. How can they not?

Soon it's a little parade of freaks, with Jimmy at the head like a drum major.

And then he takes off. *(Stage right. JIMMY leaps into the air, hovers there, and lofts another inch before landing. CLAIRE's hand at her mouth.)*

I'm peeking from behind a dumpster in my old raincoat,

My hair flat around my shoulders like a wet rat.

And I don't have anything to do with that brilliant thing in the air.

And he has even less to do with Jimmy.

Enough. I break the spell, I shake him awake

He feels small in my arms, all the people watching us.

Then his eyes open on me, ash-black, and he says "You try to keep me down..."

JIMMY. *(Overlapping.)* You try to keep me down with the scaly-skins and the black-eyed beasts but you are death. I am life and you are death.

LINDA. One should never wake people in the middle of dreams.

CLAIRE. Tomorrow we walk down the aisle and I'm *death*?

(Stage left. Linda touches CLAIRE on the knee.)

LINDA. I'll have a talk with him, lamb. *(Stage right. JIMMY sits at a vanity, applying thick white pancake makeup. He is not effeminate about it. Rather it is a solemn ritual—putting on war paint. LINDA crosses to him.)* Can you believe, the big day? Wait 'till you see Claire, like some kind of delicious multi-leveled parfait. All that organza— *(JIMMY turns to her, face shocking-white.)* Oh. *(Pause.)* Tell me my daughter's being a nervous bride. Tell me there's nothing the matter with our fine young management consultant.

JIMMY. Je ne parle pas Anglais.

(Stage left. CLAIRE putting on her wedding dress. Nervous.)

LINDA. You just have to parle enough to say "I do."

JIMMY. Je ne parle pas Anglais.

LINDA. We don't have a lot of time. Where's your tux?

JIMMY. Je ne parle de plus Anglais.

LINDA. *(Trying another tack.)* Je m'appelle Linda. That's all I remember from high school, can you believe?

JIMMY. *(Rising.)* Je suis boeff mes pas biffstek.

LINDA. Ca va bien, merci. I'm afraid that's it, my whole bag of tricks.

JIMMY. *(Very close to her, a forceful whisper.)*
Je ne suis pas biffstek.
Je suis stek sans boeuf en biff.

LINDA. Oh my my my. Ou est la Tour Eiffel?

JIMMY. *(Slapping his thighs percussively with each "si.")*
Je ne suis je un tamboure.
Je suis si si si si si si si

LINDA. *(Smoldering now.)* Un pain au chocolat, s'il vous plait!

(JIMMY is elsewhere, oblivious to the game.)

JIMMY.
Tzi tzi tzi tzi tzi tzi tzi tzi
Je suis ça suis ça suis ça je ça
ça ça ça ça ça ça ça ça ça ça

LINDA. I'm afraid I lost track.

JIMMY. I am a lullabyer, I am a singer of all songs.

LINDA. *(Mischievously.)* I thought you didn't parle Anglais, Frenchie. *(JIMMY jumps. This time he does not come down. LINDA looks up at him in awe, mouth ajar. We can see that there is music in her head. CLAIRE stomps over in full wedding dress.)* Excellent young man!

    CLAIRE. Come down come DOWN.

(CLAIRE jumps after JIMMY, her arms flailing for him. After some failed attempts, she starts to take running leaps. Not even close. She continues to jump, more and more wildly.
Sound of the Wedding March beginning.
Light fades.)

END OF THE PLAY

The Divine Fallacy

TINA HOWE

The Divine Fallacy

by
Tina Howe

premiered in March, 2000 at the
Humana Festival of New American Plays

Directed by Jon Jory
Dramaturgs: Amy Wegener and Kelly Lea Miller

Cast

Victor	Tom Nelis
Dorothy	Woodwyn Koons

Scenic Designer: Paul Owen
Costume Designer: Kevin R. McLeod
Lighting Designer: Paul Werner
Sound Designer: Martin R. Desjardins
Properties Designer: Ben Hohman
Stage Manager: Janette L. Hubert
Assistant Stage Manager: Juliet Penna

CHARACTERS

VICTOR HUGO: a photographer, late 30's
DOROTHY KISS: a writer, mid 20's

SETTING

Victor's studio in downtown Manhattan.

The Divine Fallacy

(Victor's studio in downtown Manhattan. It looks like a surreal garden blooming with white umbrellas and reflective silver screens. As the lights rise we hear the joyful bass-soprano duet, "Mit unser macht ict nichts getan." from Bach's chorale, "Ein feste Burg," BWV 80. It's a freezing day in late February.
VICTOR, dressed in black, has been waiting for DOROTHY for over an hour. There's a tentative knock at his door.)

VICTOR. Finally! *(Rushing to answer it.)* Dorothy Kiss?

(DOROTHY steps in, glasses fogged over and very out of breath. She's a mousy woman dressed in layers of mismatched clothes. An enormous coat covers a bulky sweater which covers a gauzy white dress. A tangle of woolen scarves is wrapped around her neck.)

DOROTHY. *(Rooted to the spot.)* Victor Hugo?
VICTOR. At last!
DOROTHY. I'm sorry, I'm sorry, I got lost.
VICTOR. Come in, come in.
DOROTHY. I reversed the numbers of your address.
VICTOR. We don't have much time.
DOROTHY. *(With a shrill laugh.)* I went to 22 West 17th instead of 17 West 22nd!
Hugo. I have to leave for Paris in an hour.
DOROTHY. The minute I got there, I knew something was wrong.
VICTOR. *(Looking at his watch.)* No, make that forty-five minutes.
DOROTHY. There were all these naked people milling around.

95

(Pause.) With pigeons.

> VICTOR. The spring collections open tomorrow.
> DOROTHY. They were so beautiful.
> VICTOR. It's going to be a mad house.... Come in, please....

(He strides into the studio and starts setting up his equipment.)

> DOROTHY. I didn't realize they came in so many colors.

DOROTHY.	VICTOR .
Red, green, yellow, purple ...	A tidal wave of photographers
I think they'd been dyed.	is coming from all over the world.

(Pause.)

> VICTOR. I swore last year would be my last, but a man's got to make a living, right? *(Turning to look for her.)* Hey, where did you go? *(DOROTHY waves at him from the door.)* Miss Kiss ... we've got to hurry if you want me to do this. *(DOROTHY makes a strangled sound. Guiding her into the room.)* Come in, come in.... I won't bite.
> DOROTHY. *(With a shrill laugh.)* My glasses are fogged over! I can't see a thing!

(She takes them off and wipes them with the end of one of her scarves.)

> VICTOR. Here, let me help you off with your coat.

(They go through a lurching dance as he tries to unwrap all her scarves, making her spin like a top.)

VICTOR	DOROTHY
Hold still... easy does it.	Whoops, I was just ... sorry,
Atta girl....	sorry, sorry, sorry, sorry, sorry....

(He finally succeeds. They look at each other and smile, breathing heavily.)

> VICTOR. So *you're* Daphne's sister?!
> DOROTHY. Dorothy Kiss, the *writer!*

(VICTOR struggles to see the resemblance.)

DOROTHY. I know. It's a shocker.

VICTOR. No, no....

DOROTHY. She's the top fashion model in the country, and here I am ... Miss Muskrat!

VICTOR. The more I look at you, the more I see the resemblance.

DOROTHY. You don't have to do that.

VICTOR. No really. There's something about your forehead....

DOROTHY. I take after my father. The rodent side of the family.... Small, nondescript, close to the ground....

(She makes disturbing rodent faces and sounds.)

VICTOR. You're funny.

DOROTHY. I try.

(Silence.)

VICTOR. So ....

DOROTHY. *(Grabbing her coat and lurching towards the door.)* Goodbye, nice meeting you.

VICTOR. *(Barring her way.)* Hey, hey, just a minute....

DOROTHY. I can let myself out.

VICTOR. Daphne said you were coming out with a new novel and needed a photograph for the back cover.

DOROTHY. Another time....

VICTOR. It sounded wild.

DOROTHY. Oh God, oh God....

VICTOR. Something about a woman whose head keeps falling off.

DOROTHY. This was *her* idea, not mine! I hate having my picture taken! *(Struggling to get past him.)* I hate it, hate it, hate it, hate it, hate it, hate it, hate it, hate it....

VICTOR. *(Grabbing her arm.)* She told me you might react like this.

DOROTHY. *Hate it, hate it, hate it, hate it!*

VICTOR. Dorothy, Dorothy....

(DOROTHY desperately tries to escape. VICTOR grabs her in his

arms as she continues to fight him, kicking her legs. He finally plunks her down in a chair. They breathe heavily. A silence.)

DOROTHY. Why can't you set up your camera in my brain? Bore a hole in my skull and let 'er rip. *(She makes lurid sound effects.)* There's no plainness here, but heaving oceans ringed with pearls and ancient cities rising in the mist.... Grab your tripod and activate your zoom, wonders are at hand.... Holy men calling the faithful to prayer as women shed their clothes at the river's edge. ... *Click!* Jeweled elephants drink beside them, their trunks shattering the surface like breaking glass. *Click!* Their reflections shiver and merge, woman and elephant becoming one.... Slender arms dissolving into rippling tusks, loosened hair spreading into shuddering flanks.... *Click, click, click!* Now you see them, now you don't.... A breast, a tail, a jeweled eye.... *Click!* Macaws scream over head *(Sound effect.)*, or is it the laughter of the women as they drift further and further from the shore, their shouts becoming hoarse and strange....*(Sound effect.) Click! (Tapping her temple.)* Aim your camera here, Mr. Hugo. *This* is where beauty lies.... Mysterious, inchoate and out of sight! *(Silence as VICTOR stares at her. Suddenly depressed.)* I don't know about you, but I could use a drink.

VICTOR. *(As if in a dream.)* Right, right....

DOROTHY. VICTOR?! *(Pause.)* I'd like a drink, if you don't mind!

VICTOR. Coming right up. What's your poison?

DOROTHY. Vodka, neat.

VICTOR. You got it!

(He lurches to a cabinet and fetches a bottle of vodka and a glass.)

DOROTHY. That's alright, I don't need a glass. *(She grabs the bottle and drinks an enormous amount.)* Thanks, I needed that!

VICTOR. Holy Shit!

DOROTHY. *(Wiping her mouth.)* Where are my manners? I forgot about you. *(Passing him the bottle.)* Sorry, sorry....

VICTOR. *(Pours a small amount in a glass and tips it towards her.)* Cheers!

(She raises an imaginary glass.)

DOROTHY. Could I ask you a personal question?

VICTOR. Shoot.

DOROTHY. Are you really related to Victor Hugo?

VICTOR. Strange but true.

DOROTHY. Really, really?

VICTOR. *Really!* He was my great great grandfather! *(Bowing.)* *A vôtre service.*

DOROTHY. He's my favorite writer! He's all I read.... Over and over and over again! I can't believe I'm standing in the same room with you!

(She suddenly grabs one of his cameras and starts taking pictures of him.)

VICTOR. Hey, what are you doing? That's a two thousand dollar camera you're using!

(He lunges for it. She runs from him, snapping his picture.)

DOROTHY. A direct descendent of Victor Hugo....

VICTOR. *(Chasing her.)* Put that down!

DOROTHY. *(Snapping him at crazy angles.)* No one will believe me!

VICTOR. Give it here! *(Finally catching her.)* I SAID: GIVE ME THAT CAMERA!

(They struggle. A torrent of blood gushes from her hand.)

DOROTHY. Ow! Ow!

VICTOR. *(Frozen to the spot.)* Miss Kiss.... Miss Kiss.... Oh my God, my God.... *(DOROTHY gulps for air.)* What did I do? *(Her breathing slowly returns to normal.)* Are you alright?

DOROTHY. *(Weakly.)* A tourniquet.... I need a tourniquet.

VICTOR. On the double!

(He races around looking for one.)

DOROTHY. Wait, my sock....

(She kicks off one of her boots and removes a white sock.)

VICTOR. *(Running to her side.)* Here, let me help.
DOROTHY. No, I can do it.

(She expertly ties it to stop the flow of blood.)

VICTOR. How are you feeling?
DOROTHY. Better thanks.
VICTOR. I'm so sorry.
DOROTHY. It's not your fault.
VICTOR. I didn't mean to hurt you.
DOROTHY. I have a stigmata.
VICTOR. *What?*
DOROTHY. I said I have a stigmata. It bleeds when I get wrought up.
VICTOR. *You have a stigmata?*
DOROTHY. Several, actually.
VICTOR. Jesus Christ!
DOROTHY. Jesus Christ, indeed.
VICTOR. A *stigmata*? In *my* studio?!

(Silence.)

DOROTHY. I'm afraid you're going to miss your plane to Paris. I'm sorry. *(A silence. She hands him his camera.)* Well, I guess you may as well take my picture.
VICTOR. Right, right ... your picture.

(She removes her glasses and bulky sweater and looks eerily beautiful in her white gauzy dress.)

DOROTHY. I'm as ready as I'm ever going to be. *(VICTOR is stunned, unable to move.)* Yoo hoo ... Mr. Hugo?
VICTOR. You're so beautiful!
DOROTHY. *(Lowering her eyes.)* Please!
VICTOR. You look so sad.... Like an early Christian martyr. *(A great light starts to emanate from her. VICTOR races to get his camera and begins taking her picture. Breaking down.)* I can't ... I can't ... I just ... can't.
DOROTHY. Victor, Victor, it's alright.... We all have something.... You have your eye, Daphne has her beauty and I have this.

It's OK. It makes me who I am. *(VICTOR struggles to control himself.)* Listen to me.... Listen.... When the Navahos weave a blanket, they leave in a hole to let the soul out—the flaw, the fallacy—call it what you will. It's part of the design, the most important part—faith, surrender, a mysterious tendency to bleed....

VICTOR. I'm so ashamed.

DOROTHY. You did your job. You took my picture.

VICTOR. But I didn't see you.

DOROTHY. Shh, shh....

VICTOR. I was blind.

DOROTHY. Shhhhhh....

VICTOR. *(Breaking down again.)* Blind, blind, blind....

(DOROTHY rises and places her hands over his eyes and then raises them in a gesture of benediction.)

DOROTHY. There, there, it's alright. It's over.

(The lights blaze around them as the closing measures of Bach's duet swell.)

END OF THE PLAY

Between Two Friends

STEPHEN McFEELY

Between Two Friends

by
Stephen McFeely

*premiered in August, 2001 at
Actors Theatre of Louisville*

Directed by Jennifer Hubbard
Dramaturg: Victoria Zyp

Cast

A	Eddie Kurtz
B	Celeste Den

Costume Designer: Kevin McLeod
Lighting Designer: Tony Penna
Sound Designer: Ben Marcum
Properties Designer: Tracey Rainey
Production Manager: Frazier Marsh
Stage Manager: Michael Hausladen

Oft have I digg'd up dead men from their graves,
And set them upright at their dear friends' doors,
Even when their sorrows almost were forgot;
And on their skins, as on the bark of trees,
Have with my knife carved in Roman letters,
'Let not your sorrow die, though I am dead.'

—TITUS ANDRONICUS, Act V

Between Two Friends

(Two characters: A and B. A waits on stage. B enters.)

B. Do you have a shovel?

A. Why?

B. I want to borrow it. I want to borrow you and your shovel.

A. For what?

B. Digging. With the shovel.

A. You'll have to be more specific.

B. If I tell you any more, it'll ruin the *surprise*.

A. Surprise?

B. Yes.

A. You have another one?

B. I do.

A. And you want me to go?

B. We'll might need one more person, but yes, absolutely I'd like you to go.

A. And you need me?

B. And a shovel.

A. What is it?

B. You enjoyed the last one.

A. Sure. I feel a little guilty, but yes, I enjoyed it.

B. Because of the reaction on his face.

A. And the 'whoop' sound. God, that was funny.

B. 'Whoop.'

A. 'Whoop.'

B. He never saw it coming.

A. Never saw it coming.

B. This one's better.

A. Better?

B. Sharper in focus.

A. Tell me.

B. Okay. Like last time—

A. —I'm sworn to secrecy, I know, I know.

B. All right. Here it is.... I want to go to the cemetery and dig up a body and put it on somebody's doorstep and ring the bell and run away.

A. ... Huh. Why would you want to do that?

B. Same reason we did the last one.

A. The last one was for kicks. For fun.

B. Right. Same thing.

A. Not really.

B. No?

A. No.... Not really.

B. I see them as the same.

A. Why do you want to do this?

B. Because it doesn't matter.

A. I don't think I follow.

B. I just want to do this. So I will.

A. For revenge, or something?

B. No, I don't think so.

A. Hate? Is it out of hate?

B. Maybe.

A. Evil?

B. I hope not. But I'll allow for that possibility.

A. You will?

B. I'm not exactly an innocent.

A. You want to dig up a random body and put it on somebody's doorstep and you'll allow for the possibility that it might appear evil.

B. What can I say, people judge ... and it's not a random body.

A. What's that?

B. This is all very specific.

A. Who?

B. I think you know.

A. I think I don't.

B. Arthur Pemble.

A. Oh.... Oh, God. Mr. Pemble. That was just, that was just recently.

B. March the 3rd.

A. He drowned.

B. Drowned.

A. In a, in a fishing accident.

B. Glub, glub, glub.

A. He was what, not even 40? I mean, his kids.

B. Thomas Jr., and Julie, ages 12 and 9.

A. Mrs. Pemble went on our field trips.

B. Actually, that will help. When she opens the door, we'll be able to read the look on her face, and compare it to when she was driving the van to the science museum.

A. She just must be ... well, just a wreck, all of them.

B. I know. It'll be great.

A. I'm not sure I can do that.

B. Why's that?

A. Believe it or not, I'm a little reluctant.

B. Because?

A. Because it's really fucking evil.

B. It's no different from the other ones.

A. Of course it's different from the other ones.

B. Why?

A. What do you mean, why? There's a big obvious fucking difference.

B. Don't get all excited. Explain the difference. I don't see the difference.

A. How about the other ones didn't require digging up the remains of human beings.

B. This is no different than going through the trash.

A. You're kidding, right?

B. We bury cereal boxes and old mattresses in landfills. Nobody has a hissy fit when people turn that into art.

A. Art.

B. You've seen those modern sculptures made out of junk—

A. You consider this art.

B. Yes.

A. Putting the body on the doorstep, running away, that's art.

B. Of a sort.

A. You consider the other things we've done art.

B. Not all of them. Some were better than others, but generally, yes. They were all works of art.

A. I don't see that.

B. You don't appreciate it, yet.

A. Yet.

B. I'd like to think you're learning.

A. Is that why you bring me along? To teach me?

B. And I'm hoping you have a shovel.

A. ... I don't believe I want to go.

B. Because you're insulted?

A. I'm not insulted.

B. Then why?

A. This will hurt somebody.

B. We're not *throwing* the body at them.

A. This will do damage to somebody. Maybe Mrs. Pemble. Definitely the kids— God, the kids, if they saw it.

(Pause.)

B. Maybe you're concerned for yourself?

A. Yeah. Maybe. Maybe this would do damage to me. Maybe this is a bad thing for me to do. And for you.

B. I've decided it's not.

A. Fine, then maybe I decide you do this by yourself.

B. You can do that. It doesn't matter.

A. What does that mean?

B. If I get caught, they'll assume you did it with me.

A. Why would they do that?

B. You did the other ones.

A. Are you threatening me?

B. Do you feel threatened?

A. Yes.

B. Interesting.

A. You'd own up. If you were caught you'd clear me.

B. I would?

A. Yes, you would.

B. Because I'm ... honorable?

(Pause.)

A. What I did before was not this.

B. Words. It might as well have been.

A. But it wasn't.

B. Chance.

A. No, it was my decision. I judged each one individually.

B. And went along with all of them.

A. ... Yes.

B. And it really didn't take you that long to decide, if I remember right.

A. Fine, then tonight's no different. I've decided quickly, and I've decided not to go.

B. And your reason being...?

A. I am not prepared to set this precedent.

B. Really.

A. Really.

B. "You are not prepared to set this precedent." Is that what you said.

A. Yes, why—

B. I just want to get it right.

A. This, doing this, sets a—

B. Shh, I'm thinking about what you said.... Okay. "You are not prepared to set this precedent." I have a response.

A. Do you.

B. Here is my response: Bullshit.

A. That's your response.

B. Precedent implies a pattern. A progression. First this, then that. First sugar cereal, then crack cocaine.

A. That's not what I'm talking about—

B. But that's what you're worried about. That tonight might actually go well. That you'll enjoy yourself. That you'll want to do it, or something like it, again. *(Pause.)* There are no patterns. There are *events*. If they are repeated, it's by choice. You choose to repeat them. But you choose every time. Every time a new and different choice. If you think your previous choices have any effect on anything, then, I'm sorry to say, you're an arrogant prick.

A. *I'm* an arrogant prick?

B. If you subscribe—

A. "I'm an arrogant prick." Is that what you said?

B. Yes, but—

A. I just want to get it right.

B. That is, if you believe—

A. Shh, I'm thinking on what you said.... Okay. "I'm an arrogant prick." I have a response.

B. Do you.

A. Here it is: You're an asshole!

B. You think somebody sets out to marry six women in a row who all remind him of his mother? No. It's only after the fact, after a guy's dead or in jail that *someone else* can look back on it and say "On the whole, that was pretty creepy."

A. If it's all the same—as you've said—I'll just stay here. Thank you for the invitation. No, thank you.

B. So, you're drawing a line.

A. Yes, sorry. Grave-robbing is apparently my line.

B. No, that's fine. I understand. I sympathize.

A. You sympathize.

B. It's not for everybody.

A. It's not for anybody.

B. *(Smiles.)* Not any body. Just Arthur Pemble.

A. What do you have against them?

B. The Pembles? Nothing. I've never met them.

A. Then why?

B. Because, it doesn't matter. I can. It has occurred to me, it is possible, and I want to do it.

A. And you see no repercussions.

B. What's the point in that?

A. Some thoughts should not be acted upon.

(Pause. B makes to leave.)

B. Sorry, I thought we were on the same page. I was wrong.

A. What did you think?

B. It doesn't matter. I misjudged. I apologize for getting into this with you. Good luck.

A. What did you think? Wait. What did you think I'd say?

B. No, it's not your fault—

A. Tell me.

B. It's just that I thought you were already past this.

A. This?

B. This pretend morality. This ceiling. I was wrong.

A. You mean 'Some thoughts should not be acted upon'?

B. I thought you were past that.

A. Who gets past that? That's … conscience.

B. Yeah. See, I thought you were over that.

A. Conscience.

B. Yes.

A. You thought I was over my conscience.

B. Well, yes.

A. You're over yours.

B. Definitely.

A. Got no use for it.

B. Wouldn't know where to find it if I did.

A. Huh.... So there's nothing that stops you from doing things.

B. I'm supposed to limit myself?

A. From some things.

B. I do what I want.

A. What about others?

B. You mean like Others with a capital O?

A. Your Responsibility to Others.

B. That's not my bag.

A. What's not your bag?

B. I assume you're talking about their well-being?

A. Exactly.

B. Yeah, that's not my bag. I don't wish Others be-well. I don't wish Others be-anything.

A. That's apathy.

B. Apathy is nothing. Nothing is not wrong.

A. Putting the dead body of a loved one on a grieving family's doorstep is not nothing.

B. What have I done? I've moved something. I've shifted a thing. I've rearranged furniture.

A. No.

B. I'm not killing him.

A. You're causing them pain. *(B reaches out and pinches A's arm.)* Ow!

B. There, I just caused you pain. I reached out, *touched* you, made you hurt. I'm not doing that to the Pembles.

A. There are different kinds of pain.

B. No. There aren't.

A. It's wrong.

B. According to whom?

A. According to the laws of decency.

B. Please. *(Pause.)* You did the other ones.

A. Yes.

B. Why?

A. Why did I do the other ones?

B. Yes.

A. I didn't see the harm.

B. But some of them certainly broke the laws of decency.

A. … Yes.

B. So. Why is this different?

A. I guess I don't have an argument. Other than my conscience.

B. So you don't have an argument.

(Pause.)

A. No … I don't have an argument.

B. Do you have a shovel?

(Pause.)

A. Yes. I have a shovel.

END OF THE PLAY

Night Visits

SIMON FILL

Night Visits

by
Simon Fill

premiered in January, 2000 at
Actors Theatre of Lousiville

Directed by Sullivan Canaday White
Dramaturg: Kelly Lea Miller

Cast

Tom	Tom Johnson
Emily	Rachel Burttram
Liz	Samantha Desz

Scenic Designer: Tom Burch
Lighting Designer: Andrew Vance
Costume Designer: Jessica Byrd Waters
Properties Designer: Ann Marie Morehouse
Stage Manager: Nichole A. Shuman
Assistant Stage Manager: Juliane Taylor

CHARACTERS

TOM: a second-year resident in medicine, 28
LIZ: a nurse, 27
EMILY: gentle, looks about 23

TIME

The present

LOCATION

An examination room in a hospital.

Night Visits

(A hospital examination room. White. Patient gowns hang all over. We hear wind outside. TOM lies on the examining table, asleep. Twenty-eight. In a doctor's outfit. LIZ enters. Twenty-seven. Nurse's uniform. Quiet moment to herself, then notices the gowns and TOM.)

TOM. *(Eyes closed.)* I'm not seeing patients anymore, Liz. *(Quickly, lightly, sounding upbeat and energetic.)* It's over. It's over. It's over. It's over. It's over. It's over. It's over. It's over. It's over. It's over. It's over. It's over. It's over. It's over. It's over. Do you have a problem with it being over? You better not. Is it not really over? I don't think so.

LIZ. Tom. One more. That's all.

TOM. Seeing one patient in your thirty-fifth hour of being awake is the equivalent of seeing fifteen hundred in your first.

LIZ. You can't refuse to see patients. You're a resident.

TOM. Shit. *(He gets up.)* You look … nice.

LIZ. Got a date.

TOM. Doctor?

LIZ. No.

TOM. Yes. Yes. YES! Good for *you.*

LIZ. You are such a freak. *(Looks out window.)* Windy outside.

TOM. It's a bad night.

LIZ. I know. We all do.

TOM. … What? Oh. I'm … fine.

LIZ. We all loved Katie, Tom.

TOM. Yeah. Thanks. No, I mean it.

LIZ. She was a great nurse. I wish I'd known her more.

TOM. You're okay, Liz. I hate to admit it.

(He hits her lightly on the arm.)

LIZ. You are such a freak. *(Beat.)* This patien—Doug gave her a shot of methicillin, he's busy now. Watch her ten minutes, see if she's allergic. She was ... in a car ....

TOM. Look. Katie's accident was a year ago.

LIZ. To the day.

TOM. I'm not really doing anything to this patient anyhow.

LIZ. You mean that?

TOM. *(Very dramatic.)* Have I *ever* lied to you before?

LIZ. Yeah.

TOM. No, 'bout something serious.

LIZ. Yeah.

TOM. You're—you're—you're—

(Jokingly, he grabs a tiny knee hammer.)

LIZ. You gonna test my reflexes? You are such a ...!

TOM. What!

LIZ. *(Beat. Softly, with great fondness.)* Little boy. This patient. The accident involved only her. After it, she disappeared. They found her in a church. Sitting on the floor. Surrounded herself with lit wish candles. Hundreds. She'd been there hours. When they asked her why, she said, "I'm cold." *(She gives him a chart. He stares at her.)* Emily. I know, I know. She's odd, this one. Another sweet nobody. Passed a psych consult, but otherwise, she won't talk. Here twenty-one hours. Won't leave 'til she feels she's "okay." She's a little banged up, but fine. She could go now. She won't. Bring her upstairs when you're done. *(Beat. Studies TOM with suspicion.)* No.

TOM. I'm good at this. She'll feel better. She'll leave.

LIZ. Won't work. We tried everything. Social services was called. They'll be here soon. *(Looks at robes.)* I wish we had another free room.

TOM. You didn't carry those up from a broken dryer at three in the morning.

LIZ. Dr. Pitnick, that was nice. Someday you'll make a good nurse.

TOM. I'll get her to go.

LIZ. Won't happen. *(Looks him up and down.)* You need a compliment. Badly. *(Beat.)* Serious now. You okay?

TOM. Funny. When Katie died, I prayed every night for a month.

LIZ. What about?

TOM. If I told anyone, Liz, I'd tell you. *(Lightly.)* It was very self-involved. *(Beat.)* I'm fine. Thanks. Have a good date. You're not as cute as you think you are.

LIZ. *(Smiles.)* I'll send her down. See you tomorrow.

(She exits. Pause. The sound of wind. He looks out the window. He is overcome and starting to break down. A knock. He recovers himself.)

TOM. *(Cheerful.)* Dr. Pitnick's house of optimism and laundry! *(EMILY enters. She looks about twenty-three. Gentle. Bruised face and arms. TOM grins. A quick patter. His "routine.")* Just kidding. There's no optimism here. Don't mean to be unprofessional. I expect you to stay silent. *(Looks at chart, then her arm, checking where the shot was given.)* Hope that didn't hurt too much. I hate shots. We're gonna get you to feel okay. I usually do this by showing patients how impressive they are in comparison to me. Some patients protest. For good reason. I expect you to stay silent. They call me the funny doctor. *(To self.)* This is like one of my dates in high school. *(Looks at her.)* Did I detect a glint of humanity? *(She smiles a little.)* I bet no one upstairs tried to crack you up. Their mistake. Do you feel sorry for yourself? *(She shakes her head.)* You ought to. You gotta listen to me. But if you talk to me, you get to listen to me less. 'Round here, I'm considered aversion therapy for introverts. *(Whispers.)* Of course, being the funniest doctor 'round here is a weak claim. *(Beat. Back to normal.)* Look. I know what you went through was serious. I know. I do. But sometimes when you think you're alone, when you most think that, you … aren't. *(Beat.)* Sorry. I'm expecting a lot here. I mean, it's not like you're God or anything. No offense.

(Silence. He raises his hands in surrender, looks out the window. Pause.)

EMILY. Why would I be offended you don't think I'm God? That's pretty queer.

TOM. I'm not the one who surrounded myself with wish candles in a church.

EMILY. Does that unnerve you? Dr. Tom?

TOM. How did you know my name was Tom?

EMILY. *(Mock mystical.)* Woo woo.

(Beat. She points at his name tag.)

TOM. Oh. Wow. I need some sleep. Sorry. I shouldn't say that.

EMILY. *(Lightly teasing.)* C'mon. This is all about you. *(Beat. Sincere.)* You look tired. You okay?

TOM. Great. My patient's asking me if I'm okay. Are you?

EMILY. You want me to leave, don't you?

TOM. I .... *(Looks at her face and arms. Gentle.)* These bruises'll disappear on their own in a few days. They hurt?

EMILY. No, they feel great. Sorry. Not that bad. Thanks. You're nice.

TOM. I'm only nice when I'm tired.

EMILY. How often you tired?

TOM. Always. You're gonna be fine.

EMILY. I'm not important. What?

TOM. Nothing.

EMILY. What?

TOM. *(Warmly ironic.)* I *WISH* someone'd said that in your chart!

(She smiles.)

EMILY. You're weird.

TOM. I know.

EMILY. When the accident happened, I hit a divider, everything stopped. I didn't know where I was. For some reason, I thoughta my dad. He died four years ago. Nothing to do with cars. I ... loved him. After he was gone, I never felt his loss. I .... Something happened.

(Pause.)

TOM. You tell anyone this?

EMILY. Do you count? *(Beat.)* I got out of the car, looked around to make sure no one was hurt. Then I ran. *(Silence.)* You all right?

TOM. Yeah. Sure. I'm gonna get you outta here. In good shape.

EMILY. I'm a nobody. And I dress poorly.

TOM. What's the one thing you could do to give your life meaning?

EMILY. Accessorize? *(Beat. He smiles. She looks off.)* You can't see wind.

TOM. What?

EMILY. You can't see it, but it's there.

TOM. *(Beat.)* Is it? When the accident happened, who were you with?

EMILY. That's an odd question.

TOM. Who were you with?

EMILY. Why?

TOM. Answer it!

EMILY. No one! *(Beat.)* I was hurt, and for the first time I felt, *knew*, I'm with no one. My father, he's really ... gone.... *(Pause.)* You understand what I'm saying?

TOM. *(Thinks with care, then nods slowly.)* I'm sorry. *(Beat.)* You okay?

EMILY. *(Upset. Snippy.)* With doctors like you, who needs accidents!

TOM. Sorry.

EMILY. I .... No, don't feel bad for me. I don't. My father ... I loved him.

TOM. Did he love you?

EMILY. Yes, but that's not as important.

TOM. You okay?

EMILY. Keep asking that, and you won't be.

TOM. *(Softly.)* Sorry.

EMILY. Stop apologizing, you didn't kill him. *(Beat.)* When I left the accident, a few blocks away I passed a homeless woman. I asked her for the nearest good church. One that was honest, that wasn't about exclusion. She said nothing. I asked again, and she goes, "Here."

(She points to her heart.)

TOM. *(Softly.)* Oh.

EMILY. You enjoy helping this nobody?

TOM. Who? You?

EMILY. You know a lot about this. *(Beat.)* Who was it?

TOM. You're my patient.

EMILY. So. There's doctor-patient privilege. I won't tell anyone.

TOM. I'm trying to make *you* all right.

EMILY. You're almost there. This'll help. Or don't you open up to nobodies?

TOM. Is this a trick?

EMILY. Yes. You got me to like you.

TOM. *(Beat.)* My wife Katherine. She was a nurse here in pediatrics. We grew up together in Brooklyn, but in high school I was too shy to ask her out. We ran into each other when she'd graduated from college, at a reading of James Joyce by an Irish actor. Joyce was her favorite writer. She and I dated. At that point, I was well on my way to becoming the "funny doctor." She was quiet and funnier, in that good way the most serious people are. After two months, I proposed. Now that was funny. She didn't answer. We kept dating. Every day for two months after that I proposed. Silence. I thought, "This woman either likes me or is totally insensate." At the end of that time she gave me a copy of *Finnegans Wake,* her favorite book. At college I'd read it and almost finished. The first page, that is. But I loved her so much I slogged through the book. Boy, did I love her. On page fifty, at the bottom, in pencil, someone'd written something. I looked closely. It said, "Yes. I'll marry you." *(Pause.)* I called her up and told her Joyce had accepted my proposal of marriage. *(Pause.)* She was driving to Riverdale, a favor, to pick up a friend's kid at school. I know she was starting to think about children herself. She said she wanted them to have "my looks and her sense of humor." Another car, an old lady who shouldn't have been driving, who had a history of epilepsy … and … you know the rest. The other woman lived. *(Beat.)* I asked Katie once why she wrote "yes" to me on page fifty. She said, "I knew you loved me, but I wasn't sure how much." *(Pause.)* Don't look so serious.

EMILY. *(Gently.)* The line you draw between yourself and other people, it doesn't exist. Not how you think. You know that, you'll let her inside of you, even if she's gone.

TOM. *(Softly.)* Hey. Thanks.

EMILY. *(With affection.)* You gonna believe that? Or are you just another punk doctor?

(Long pause.)

TOM. Yeah, I do. *(Beat.)* Yeah. *(Beat.)* What do you charge? I don't know if my insurance covers this.

EMILY. This was good.

TOM. I can't treat you for premature nostalgia. It isn't my specialty. You gonna stay or go?

EMILY. Quiet in here.

TOM. *(Light. Gentle.)* That tough being a nobody? *(She smiles.)* Funny. When Katie died, I prayed every night for a month. It was very self-involved.

EMILY. No, it was just about her. You asked that she be okay. You never worried about yourself. That's incredibly rare, even for people who love each other. *And* you're a non-believer.

TOM. *(Beat.)* How'd you know that?

EMILY. Who listens to prayers?

TOM. Nobody! *(Beat. A slow realization.)* Nobody. You could leave the hospital now.

EMILY. Thanks for the permission. *(She gathers her things.)* Oh, and Tom?

TOM. Yeah?

EMILY. Your insurance doesn't cover it.

(She leaves. Pause. The sound of wind. He looks out the window. He opens it. When the wind enters the room, the robes fill with air, as if inhabited by ghosts. They sway beautifully. Tableau. Blackout.)

END OF THE PLAY

Two Truths and a Lie

MARY MICHAEL WAGNER

Two Truths and a Lie

by
Mary Michael Wagner

*premiered in August, 2000 at
Actors Theatre of Lousiville*

Directed by Trish Salerno
Dramaturg: Emily Roderer

<u>Cast</u>

Claire	Jamie L. Fish
Danny	David Strattan White

Costume Designer: Julianne Johnson
Lighting Designer: Tony Penna
Sound Designer: Dave Preston
Properties Designer: Doc Manning
Stage Manager: Emily Brauer

CHARACTERS

CLAIRE, early thirties.
DANNY, early thirties.

SETTING

New York City.
Three steps leading up to a Soho apartment.
Dusk.

Two Truths and a Lie

(A man, carrying a bag of groceries, and a woman, both out of breath, run on from opposite sides of stage and tag stair railing at the same time.)

CLAIRE. First!

DANNY. It was a tie.

CLAIRE. I should get some kind of handicap 'cause of my heels.

DANNY. Well, I've got five cantaloupes in here. *(Indicates bag.)*

CLAIRE. Fine. It's a tie.

DANNY. It's my turn to go first.

CLAIRE. Who's stopping you?

DANNY. Okay. *(Cracks knuckles. Concentrating, counts off following on his fingers.)* Last night I fed the ducks. *(Slight pause.)* I bought an Italian sausage. *(Slight pause.)* I was in bed by ten.

CLAIRE. Let's see.... Never can resist the duckees. *(Slight pause.)* You fed the ducks. Truth. You bought the sausage. Truth. The lie is that you were in bed by ten.

DANNY. I'm a vegetarian, why would I buy a sausage?

CLAIRE. Maybe so you could throw me off.

DANNY. You think I'd buy a sausage 'cause of a stupid game?

CLAIRE. You weren't in bed by ten. That's a lie. I ran into your brother uptown. He said you crashed at his place and stayed up all night blaring war documentaries.

DANNY. Foul. That's insider information.

CLAIRE. All I have to do is spot the lie, which I did. One point for me. *(With a flourish, she hops up a step.)* He said he wishes we'd get back together.

DANNY. He's just scared I'm gonna leave some kind of permanent imprint on his designer couch.

CLAIRE. If you don't play smarter you're gonna end up on his designer couch again tonight. *(Slight pause.)* My turn. One. In high school I gave my boyfriend mononucleosis. *(Slight pause.)* Two. I just got a tattoo. *(Slight pause.)* Three. I've never been kissed in an elevator.

DANNY. *(Laughing.)* You kissed me in an elevator.

CLAIRE. I never kissed you in a—

DANNY. *(Interrupting.)* On the way down ... the first day we met. *(Beat. Accusing.)* Claire.

CLAIRE. Well, if I did, it was some kind of pecky, accidental thing. I'm talking about passionate, focused making out.

DANNY. There was tongue.

CLAIRE. There was your imagination. I've never made out with you or anybody else in an elevator, okay? *(Slight pause.)* There, gave you a freebie truth. So, what's the lie.... The tattoo? Or did I give my boyfriend mono?

DANNY. You hate needles. There's no tattoo.

CLAIRE. No step for you, Buddyboy. What kind of girl do you think I am? You think I'd infect my boyfriend with mononucleosis? No wonder we broke up. You always expect the worst from me. Like the time you came home from work and all the furniture was piled by the door and—

DANNY. *(Interrupting.)* All *my* furniture. Anybody would have been suspicious.

CLAIRE. I never should have gotten you that piano. It takes up half the living room.

DANNY. I love that piano. *(Slight pause.)* Especially when I used to play and you'd lie naked underneath and tell me how the vibration of the strings would—

CLAIRE. *(Interrupting.)* It's your turn.

DANNY. So ... um ... where is it?

CLAIRE. What?

DANNY. The tattoo.

CLAIRE. Someplace ... private. *(Slight pause.)* Kind of south ... east.

DANNY. Oh. *(Inhale. Pause.)* Okay ... today I helped a guy push his smoking car out of the road. I accidentally lit my shoe on fire. *And* I masturbated while listening—

CLAIRE. *(Interrupting.)* Do I have to hear this?

DANNY. No censorship—that's *your* rule. I masturbated while listening to Wagner's *Ride of the Valkyeries*.

(He hums a few bars of the opera and makes suggestive motions with his hands.)

CLAIRE. You helped push the guy's car out of the road. Truth. *(DANNY begins humming and gesturing again.)* Oh, *that* I'm sure is true. *(Pause.)* You didn't light your shoe on fire.
DANNY. I *could* have.
CLAIRE. Obviously. *(Hops up a step.)* But you didn't.
DANNY. You can't take that step. It's against the rules to proceed until I tell you that you're right. Do you see how presumptuous you are?

(CLAIRE walks back down a step.)

CLAIRE. Well?
DANNY. *Now* you can take your step.

(She shoots him a look, takes her step.)

CLAIRE. I'm interviewing for a job in LA. I'm wearing a thong. I speak *French.
DANNY. *(Laughing.)* You don't speak French.
CLAIRE. I have mysteries, things you don't know anything about.
DANNY. *(Still laughing.)* I lived with you for five years. *(Slight pause. She begins to speak rapidly in French.)* Did you listen to tapes or something?
CLAIRE. I took three years in college, even studied in France for a month.
DANNY. How could I not know that?
CLAIRE. Maybe I was withholding it all this time so I could take this one single step.
DANNY. That would be insane.
CLAIRE. Possibly. But one more step and the apartment's mine tonight and you're back on your brother's couch.

(She hops up a step.)

DANNY. You hate LA. It's got earthquakes and riots and mud slides. Your hair'd get frizzy.

---

*This can be any language the actor knows.

CLAIRE. I didn't interview for a job in LA. That was the lie.

DANNY. *(Relieved. Slight pause.)* Look, can't we both just stay here tonight? *(He sidles up onto step she's on. Nuzzles her.)* You won't even know I'm there. I have a package of peanut butter crackers. I'll just much them quietly, then sack out on the couch.

CLAIRE. *(He's getting to her.)* We know how that always ends up.

DANNY. Yeah, last time in the bathtub. *(Pause, more nuzzling.)* You're wearing a thong?

CLAIRE. Let's stay focused.

DANNY. Claire, this is crazy. We've gotta figure out a better way to decide who's gonna sleep in the apartment than race each other home and play this insane game if there's a tie. *(Slight pause.)* I almost got hit by a bus trying to beat you home today.

CLAIRE. Give up the apartment then.

DANNY. Why don't we each take it for three days? Something normal.

CLAIRE. Where's the sport in that?

DANNY. Can't we just stop with the games?

CLAIRE. You were the one that dared me to go up in that elevator the first day we met.

DANNY. See, you remember that kiss.

CLAIRE. I remember the elevator, thinking it didn't have any music. Then thinking I couldn't even remember being on an elevator that had music.

DANNY. That's what you were thinking.

CLAIRE. I'm around heights, that's what I do, think things like that.

DANNY. Don't feel bad, I'm afraid of depths.

CLAIRE. That's exactly what you said. We were laughing. And the higher we went, I started thinking, "If the elevator shoots through the roof I won't care."

DANNY. But your hand was shaking when you pulled the knob to stop the elevator so you could kiss me.

CLAIRE. I wasn't ….

DANNY. When the elevator started going again, going down, my knees and my stomach … I … it's almost like now I think that's how I should always feel after I kiss somebody.

CLAIRE. *(Softly.)* I think you should take your turn. It's gonna get dark soon, you should—

DANNY. One. When I was a kid I tried to get in the Guinness Book of World Records by eating pennies. Two. My boss yelled at me today. *(Pause.)* Three. I'm still in love with you.

CLAIRE. Fuck you, Danny. That's against the rules.

DANNY. No censorship. Your rule.

CLAIRE. You never ate any pennies.

DANNY. Half a roll. Which one's the lie, Claire?

CLAIRE. You won the point.

DANNY. Don't you want to know the truth?

CLAIRE. You won, just take your step.

DANNY. But don't you wanna know whether I'm still in love with you or if my boss yelled at me today? Which ones seems more *(Slight pause.)* likely? The yelling or the loving?

CLAIRE. *(Overlapping.)* Take your step.

DANNY. Which one? The yelling or the loving? The yelling or the loving?

CLAIRE. *(Overlapping last line, counting off on her fingers.)* This morning I had a temperature. I stepped on a piece of chewing gum in the subway. *(Beat, voice breaks imperceptibly.)* When I was a kid my cousin Billy held me down once, and I let him break my arm rather than say "uncle."

DANNY. *(Soft voice.)* God. That's the saddest thing I ever heard. I—Claire?

CLAIRE. *(Beat. Not looking at him.)* That's the lie.

DANNY. *(Shakes his head, disbelieving. Beat.)* Okay, Claire, you're a competitor, right? Did my boss yell or am I still in love with you? Guess correctly and the whole thing is yours—bay windows, moldy shower curtain, piano, cat, everything.

(DANNY slides his keys out of his pocket and waves them around.)

CLAIRE. What are you saying?

DANNY. Guess correctly and the apartment is all yours. Forever.

CLAIRE. This isn't how we play

DANNY. Come on, Claire. *(Shakes keys.)* Neither one of us will ever have to wait around the corner to see when the other one's coming so we can make it a tie. I've seen your bangs sticking out from around the corner of the building. *(Points.)*

CLAIRE. Have not.

DANNY. Don't you think it's a coincidence how often we tie?

And then we have to go through this game. It's like foreplay, you telling me about your tattoo, your little thong. We might as well be ripping each other's cloths off.

CLAIRE. I'm just fighting for a warm place to sleep.

DANNY. You're saying you've never ever, *ever* waited around that corner so you could tie—so you could ... flirt with ... be close to me?

CLAIRE. And risk losing?

DANNY. This is your last chance, Claire. I'm not playing around now, do you understand? *(Pause.)* You're telling me that you've never waited behind that building right there until you saw me coming? *(Slight pause. CLAIRE shakes her head.)* That's your final answer then? *(CLAIRE nods. DANNY walks a few steps away from apartment then walks back. Jangles keys.)* Let's finish the game. For the whole enchilada. Which is the lie—the loving or the yelling? No more standing out here on cold nights. No more crashing on friends' couches. No more racing home from work dragging groceries in the rain.

CLAIRE. You are breaking the rules.

DANNY. For the whole apartment. You can end it right here, right now.

CLAIRE. Let's just finish the game the way we always do.

DANNY. Come on. Which is it?

(DANNY jangles the keys.)

CLAIRE. You can have the apartment tonight, okay, I'll ... I'll stay over at—

DANNY. *(Interrupting. Yelling.)* Come on, Claire, Which one? It's your fucking game. Now play!

CLAIRE. *(Yelling.)* The lie is that you're still in love with me. There. *(He grips the keys in his hand and looks at his closed fist. Then he unfolds his fingers and holds the keys out to her. Confused.)* What?

DANNY. Bull's-eye.

(He hands her the keys.)

CLAIRE. What do you ...?

DANNY. Guess you got me.

CLAIRE. I ....

DANNY. Look, I've got the morning off tomorrow, I'll come by then and get my stuff.

(DANNY starts to leave.)

CLAIRE. Where are you going?
DANNY. *(Turns back.)* You won.
CLAIRE. You forgot your groceries.
DANNY. You keep that too, that way, you'll have everything.

(DANNY exits. CLAIRE turns to door, inserts key. DANNY disappears offstage. CLAIRE turns key, but does not enter house. Instead, she turns back around and sits down on front stoop.
Blackout.)

END OF THE PLAY

Day of Our Dead

ELAINE ROMERO

In memory of Carolyn Joyce Eggers

Day of Our Dead

by
Elaine Romero

was co-commissioned by
Playwrights Theatre of New Jersey
(John Pietrowski, Artistic Director)
and The Working Theatre
(Robert Arcaro and Mark Plesent, Artistic Directors).

It was produced Off-Broadway in June 2001 at
The Working Theatre as part of a group of
one-acts entitled Free Market.

Directed by Joseph Megel
Dramaturg: Emily Franzosa

Cast

Ana	Lourdes Martin
Cindy	Constance Boardman

Set Designer: Dean Taucher
Costume Designer: Cindy Capraro
Lighting Designer: Jeff Koger
Stage Manager: Sue Semaan
Composer: Michael Keck
Production Manager: Alan Kerr
Casting: Jerry Beaver

Produced in association with
Publicity Outfitters, Timothy Haskell

CHARACTERS

ANA: A *curandera*, a traditional Mexican folk healer.
CINDY: An Anglo woman from the Midwest in her late 20's or 30's.

SETTING

The Sonoran desert.
An outdoor courtyard in the middle of nowhere.
The present.

Day of Our Dead

(Off a desert trail, and amidst the saguaro cactus, an old sign reads: limpias $15, herbal remedios $25. Before an altar full of religious candles and items built into a crumbling adobe wall sits ANA, a curandera, a Mexican healer. In front of her sit bundles of sage, rosemary, and yerba buena. As she ties the bundles with a string, she exchanges breath with each bundle before she hangs it up to dry in the sun. A pair of men's tennis shoes sits on her altar. She smudges the shoes with sage. It's a private moment— sad.
CINDY wanders in, dressed for a hike.)

CINDY. I got desperately lost. Hiking.

ANA. I am the definition of desperation.

CINDY. Herbs, right!

ANA. My bird's late. He's supposed to announce my guests, so I'm not bothered while I'm working.

(ANA stares her down. CINDY shakes her head.)

CINDY. I was just taking a walk.

ANA. *(Beat.)* Remember. *(CINDY doesn't get it.)* What you want to forget.

CINDY. I don't know what I want to forget. I must have forgotten.

(CINDY starts to leave.)

ANA. We must face these things. No matter how hard—

CINDY. Healing herbs. Magic. I don't buy this. I don't buy you.

ANA. *Pues,* don't buy. My bird'll lead you out. Spirits come out at dusk—tonight. Isn't that why you're here?

(CINDY drops her head, unsure of her mission.)

CINDY. I don't know why I'm here.

(CINDY looks like she might go.)

ANA. If you don't believe, nothing happens. The bird'll lead you out. *(CINDY hesitates.)* Has something—happened?
CINDY. No. *(ANA stares her down.)* No.
ANA. Hard to work out alone. Isn't that why you're here?
CINDY. Look, I—
ANA. Something has happened.
CINDY. I should've learned my lesson about Arizona by now. I stepped on a cactus yesterday. And this woman came out of nowhere and removed it with a hair pick and I just started crying. Because it hurt.
ANA. And then?
CINDY. There is no then. That's the whole story.
ANA. And, then.
CINDY. *(Beat.)* And, then I saw him. And I'm really not supposed to see him anymore. But he was there. Speaking. With his low low voice. From cigarettes. And that laugh. That laugh once gone never to be replaced. And then, just vanished. Like he was supposed to be. For real.
ANA. Sit. *(CINDY sits. ANA hands her a rock. CINDY senses something strange about the rock. CINDY pushes the rock away. ANA hands her the rock again, but she won't take it.)* It's just a rock. From the earth. Nothing to be afraid of.

(ANA slowly hands CINDY the rock. She takes it. It seems to affect her.)

CINDY. I ... I ....
ANA. Shhh.

(CINDY takes a deep breath.)

CINDY. I see ... things now. Since I got here. And when I left is when it happened. And ... it sort of made me feel like it was my fault.

ANA. Do you believe it was your fault?

(CINDY puts the rock down.)

CINDY. *(Upbeat at first.)* I bought myself this cute little adobe house in *(Bad Spanish)* Barrio Viejo. Real adobe. From the earth. *(Excited)* I had to outbid another woman to get it. The family there, they'd painted my house in really really bright colors, but it fit. When you see things. Against the desert. They look sharper.

ANA. More real.

CINDY. Anyway, I heard things—in that house. Ghosts. It'd belonged to this old Mexican family for like a hundred years. That family told me their dead may still come and visit on the Day of the Dead. "Our dead might get lost and come to see you." *(Quick beat.)* That might just freak me out. If that were to happen. The dead, you see, they don't come. Once our dead are dead, they're dead. They rest in peace with the angels, right? "They know not anything."

(ANA moves her hands around CINDY's head, sweeping her aura.)

ANA. It's my work—to make you better. Your work's to relax.

CINDY. What's that you're doing? Really soothing—like water in the bay. *(Long beat.)* I've seen him—several times in that house, but I always close my eyes—to block him out.

ANA. You weren't scared of him in life. Why be scared of him now?

CINDY. He's been visiting, actually ... my dead father. In the night when I'm half asleep.

ANA. Your father isn't visiting to bother you.

CINDY. But he's still hanging around. And that does bother me.

ANA. It's that day. *El día de los muertos.* The Day of the Dead. You knew it when you sought me out.

CINDY. I didn't—

ANA. You had the man on the trail mark your map. You ....

CINDY. Yes.

ANA. Yes.

CINDY. I can't leave him—to rest in peace with the angels. There is no peace. When you don't say "goodbye."

(ANA burns some herbs. CINDY looks questioningly.)

    ANA. It clears things out.
    CINDY. Don't send him away.
    ANA. Now, get his favorite things. You have them in that bag. Take them out.

(A beat. CINDY reaches into her bag, pulls out a pack of cigarettes, matchboxes, and a dozen donuts. She places them on the altar, ending with a cup of Dunkin' Donuts' coffee.)

    CINDY. Half the coffee spilled out on the way over, but it's his favorite. That family told me this is what you do. You guys get stuff the person liked for the altar. Smokes, some guy's shoes. Weird. Put them there or at their gravesite …. *(ANA motions for CINDY to put the cup on the altar.)* Kind of silly, but ….

(ANA motions for CINDY to pray. CINDY can't.)

    ANA. Your father would have liked this, to see you create something.
    CINDY. Yes, yes, an atheist. Finding abhorrence and hypocrisy in the church, saying we don't go anywhere when we die. Saying he would just crumble into dust. Liar.
    ANA. He would like this then.
    CINDY. His things. His habits.
    ANA. Yes.
    CINDY. I'm—
    ANA. *(Beat.)* Stay. I dare you. I see a competitive streak. And a gift.

(CINDY nods in agreement. She drops her head and starts fidgeting. She picks up the rock ANA gave her earlier; she begins to focus.)

    CINDY. *(Long beat)* I might know what he's trying to tell me. I might be hearing his voice right now. How does an atheist have the gall to come like a ghost?
    ANA. Spirits learn things on the other side … that they didn't know in life.
    CINDY. Like?

ANA. How to say, "I'm sorry, Cindy. I wasn't what you wanted, but I did love you."

CINDY. Stuff like that?

ANA. Stuff like that.

(CINDY lights the herb ANA lit earlier and starts to cleanse herself with the smoke.)

CINDY. And then there are the simple things. I'd like to know he'd answer if I called. If I could call.

ANA. Knowing what he knows now, he would.

CINDY. Aren't you just making shit up? I can make shit up, too. Like these tennis shoes. What do they have to do with God?

ANA. I share this space with you out of the goodness of my soul.

CINDY. Well, it doesn't work.

ANA. Then, leave. Since it doesn't work.

CINDY. Does it happen very often—that the last communication you have with someone you love is a fight?

ANA. Don't touch the offerings, *gringa. (Beat.)* My son's shoes.

CINDY. *(Dawning on her.)* Oh, you mean your son's— *(dead).* I'm sorry.

ANA. Those shoes—the subject of a very hateful fight. And then Lalo got in his car and sped away because I had made him very angry. He drove out to the desert. The road turned. He didn't. "I never want to see you again." Those were my last words. If there's some healing, some prayers I can say to help—

CINDY. I am sorry. For your loss. *(Beat.)* Is your son going to come back when the sun goes down?

(They sit beside each other as dusk descends.)

ANA. It's good to remember. Our dead.

CINDY. *(Grabbing ANA's hand.)* I like your work.

ANA. If you tell your eye not to look, you can get a peek of what's really there. I see the potential in you.

CINDY. When I was a little girl, I wanted to be a nurse. *(CINDY hands ANA the rock. She takes it for a moment.)* I wanted to help people. I still feel that impulse inside me.

(ANA hands CINDY back the rock.)

ANA. No.

(CINDY places the rock in ANA's hand and cups ANA's hand over it.)

CINDY. Nothing to be afraid of. Just part of the earth. All the magic happens after dusk.

ANA. This kind of work. It takes years to master. You insult me with these feeble efforts—

CINDY. To heal you?

ANA. Nothing's going to—

CINDY. Happen? If you believe, something might. Here. *(CINDY closes ANA's eyes.)* Close your eyes and picture Lalo in your head really good. And when you have that picture firm, with his tennis shoes on. When you imagine him in a way you can't forget, smiling, let yourself feel him here. In this place with us. *(Beat.)* Can you ... sense him? Lalo?

(ANA does.)

ANA. I'm—

CINDY. You weren't scared of him in life. Why be scared of him now? *(ANA laughs. CINDY ignites the herbs and cleanses them both with the smoke.)* Here. I'll bring my dad, too. We'll gather everybody here. *(She takes a moment.)* Oh, I see ... my father. My father says, "Cindy, I'm not a man of many words, but I just want to say—I just want to say, I forgive you—"

ANA. *(Simultaneously.)* I forgive you.

CINDY. I forgive you. I forgive *you,* Daddy. *(Beat.)* And he just stands there and holds my hand. And then, he lets it go really slowly, like a kiss. That's all he had to say. And thanks for the coffee. I'm waving and waving, like an idiot, waving goodbye. My father walks right past your son. Lalo's been standing here quietly this whole time. He wants to be in your presence, he says. He remembers admiring you in this courtyard when he was a little boy. He'd look in—

ANA. And smile

CINDY. They love us, Ana. From far far away. They came back to see us all the way from the dead. That means a lot—to take a journey like that. *(CINDY slowly opens her eyes.)* That's all I see.

ANA. *Te doy gracias.*

CINDY. No, thank you.

(They both stare at the altar as if wanting more as lights go to black.)

END OF THE PLAY

Guys

ROBB BADLAM

Guys

by
Robb Badlam

premiered in 1996 at the
Indigo Jones Coffee House
in New Brunswick, New Jersey

Directed by Mark Piotrowski

Cast

Duff	George L. Smith III
Ty	Rafael DeOliviera

SETTING

Where: A booth at McDonalds.

When: Any day, really.

Guys

(A booth at McDonalds. DUFF and TY are eating quietly. Both men are in their early 20's. They are reasonably good looking—TY somewhat more so than DUFF. They are reasonably unkempt— DUFF somewhat more so than TY. Both men are in college. TY has a newspaper open and is intently scrutinizing it. DUFF is staring off, thinking. They munch their fries for a long thoughtful moment. Then a contemplative bite of burger. Repeat. The silent chewing goes on for a bit.)

DUFF. You know what I really like, Ty?
TY. *(Not looking up.)* What's that, Duff?
DUFF . Breasts.
TY. Sure.

(Pause.)

DUFF. I mean it. I'm really very fond of them.
TY. Okay.

(Pause.)

DUFF. Not too big, not too small. Just a good, round breast.
TY. Roundness is key.
DUFF. And firmness. Somewhere between a water balloon and a Nerf ball.
TY. It's important.

(Pause.)

DUFF. I had a dream once. I was totally naked. Barefoot. Walking through this huge field of naked breasts.

TY. What'd you do?

DUFF. I fell down a lot. *(Pause. Indicates a tray liner or poster with his French fry.)* You suppose Mayor McCheese gets laid?

TY. Hmm?

DUFF. Mayor McCheese.

TY. Yep.

DUFF. How you figure?

TY. He's the mayor.

(Pause.)

DUFF. But he's got a big freakish head full of soggy meat.

TY. Never underestimate the allure of celebrity.

DUFF. The allure of celebrity?

TY. Dude, people have sex with Steve Buscemi.

(Pause.)

DUFF. You suppose anybody ever just goes up to him and takes a big bite out of his face?

TY. Steve Buscemi?

DUFF. Mayor McCheese. He *is* a big cheeseburger. You think anybody ... you know ... bites him?

TY. *(Irritated.)* No.

DUFF. Why?

TY. *(Finally looking up from his paper.)* Dude. He's the *mayor.*

(Pause.)

DUFF. What are you reading?

TY. Crossword.

DUFF. You're *reading the* crossword?

TY. I'm *doing* the crossword.

DUFF. But you're not writing anything down.

TY. I'm doing it in my head.

DUFF. In your head.

TY. Yeah. *(Beat.)* It's pretty hard.

(Pause.)

DUFF. Why are you doing it in your head?
TY. Lost my pen.

(Pause.)

DUFF. You could use another pen.
TY. Don't have another pen.

(Pause.)

DUFF. You could borrow someone else's pen.
TY. I liked my pen.

(Pause.)

DUFF. You could buy a new pen.
TY. *(Squinting at the page.)* That's a lot a trouble to go through just for a crossword, dude.

(Pause.)

DUFF. So ... you lost your pen and now you're gonna go the whole rest of your life without writing anything down?
TY. It's not much of a plan, but it'll do for now.

(Pause.)

DUFF. You know what we need, Ty?
TY. Girlfriends, Duff?
DUFF. *(Sighing.)* Yeah. *(TY returns to his crossword. DUFF returns to his fries. Suddenly DUFF perks up as he notices something off stage. NOTE: It's important that we never see the young lady in question.)* Dude. Dude. Five o'clock.
TY. My five or yours?
DUFF. Yours. *(TY takes a moment to figure out where five o'clock is, then moves to turn. DUFF stops him.)* Wait! Not yet!
TY. What's the recon?
DUFF. No visible rings. No apparent male accompaniment.
TY . And for lunch... ?
DUFF. I believe she's selected the McNuggets.

TY. Solid menu choice.
DUFF. Okay. She's not looking.

(TY turns, trying not to be obvious but doing a terrible job of it. He grabs a handful of Duff's fries and tosses them over his shoulder. He then turns to pick it up. He looks in her direction as he retrieves the fries from the floor.)

TY. *(Impressed.)* Ka-Blammo.

(TY pops some floor fries into his mouth.)

DUFF. Hear, hear. *(Pause.)* You know, if women could spend just half an hour inside a male brain ... just half an hour ... they'd never talk to us again.
TY. They don't talk to us now.
DUFF. No, I mean all of us. Men. They'd cut us off completely. Because they'd finally figure out that fully one half of the male brain is constantly masturbating. We can't help it. It just happens. It's nature.
TY. Like photosynthesis.
DUFF. Completely independent of our higher brain activities. And it's not just your leering construction workers of the world. It's all guys.
TY. Everybody.
DUFF. Albert Einstein. Probably thinking: E equals MC—I wanna wear your ass like a sombrero—squared. Couldn't help it.
TY. He's a guy.
DUFF. You're damn skippy.

(Pause.)

TY. My dad always says he wants to come back in the next life as a woman's bicycle seat.
DUFF. Your dad has some things he needs to work out, dude. *(Pause)* Ty.
TY. Hmm.
DUFF. She has a pen.

(Brightening, TY emerges from his crossword.)

TY. My pen?

DUFF. No. *(TY, disappointed, returns to his crossword.)* Ask her if you can borrow it.

TY. But it's not my pen.

DUFF. Dude. Work with me here ....

TY. Even if it *was* my pen, I couldn't borrow it. You can't borrow things that already belong to you....

DUFF. Dude! Focus!

TY. Oh. *(Beat.)* An "in"?

DUFF. Hallelujah!

TY. That's a high difficulty maneuver, dude.

DUFF. Opportunity is knocking, my friend. You have an in! She has a pen. You need a pen. It couldn't be more perfect!

TY. Why don't *you* ask her.

(Pause.)

DUFF. *(Caught, deer in the headlights.)* I don't *need* a pen. *(Pause)* Take off your watch.

TY. What?

DUFF. Take off your watch.

TY. Why?

DUFF. So you can ask her what time it is.

TY. Why don't you?

DUFF. I'm not wearing a watch. *(TY blinks at him, trying to make sense that.)* Shut up, Ty.

TY. If *you* want to talk to her, why do you want *me* to go over?

DUFF. You'll be my facilitator.

TY. Facilitator.

DUFF. You know. Break the ice. Little small talk. "Say, that's a damn nice pen. Pens are cool. I really like pens." Then I join in. "I had a pen once." You get things started. Like a warm-up band.

TY. A warm-up band.

DUFF. Yes.

TY. No. *(TY returns to his crossword. DUFF is eating himself alive. He really wants to talk to this woman, but is powerless. Sensing his anxiety, TY looks up.)* Would you just *go*.

DUFF. What?

TY. Just go over there and introduce yourself.

DUFF. You're real brave when it's somebody else's neck on the line.

TY. What neck? There's no neck. This is a neck-free situation. Worst she can do? Say no.

DUFF. *(Becoming frantic.)* Me? Go over there? Without an in? That's *exactly* what she'll do! And where does that leave me? Standing in the middle of McDonalds! Pen-less! Watch-less! And completely emasculated!

(Pause.)

TY. You've thought about this a lot, haven't you. *(They sit a moment in silence.)* Fifty bucks.

DUFF. Huh?

TY. It's yours. Fifty bucks. You go over there, say: "hello." She says: "No thanks." ... "I have a boyfriend." ... "Eat mace and die, freak-boy." ... Shoots you down in any way—there's fifty bucks in it for you. To soften the blow.

DUFF. Where are you going to get fifty bucks.

TY. I'll sell a kidney. Fifty bucks.

DUFF. *(Considering.)* What if she says yes? *(TY sighs and shakes his head in frustration. He returns to his crossword. They sit in silence.)* I can't.

TY. Why not?

(DUFF has no answer.)

DUFF. *(Quietly)* Because?

TY. Fifty American dollars.

(Pause.)

DUFF. And all I have to do is go over there.

TY. Just go over there.

DUFF. And say hello.

TY. And say hello.

(Pause.)

DUFF. I don't know .... *(TY quietly begins making chicken clucking noises.)* Oh that's not fair!

TY. Fifty bucks.

DUFF. Not enough.

TY. Well, how about fifty bucks and whatever's left of your dignity?

DUFF. Hmm....

TY. *(Returning to his crossword.)* Didn't think so.

DUFF. You don't believe I can introduce myself to a woman?

TY. Nope.

DUFF. I'll have you know I am very good at making conversation. I have talked to many, *many* women in my life.

TY. Cashiers. Waitresses. The occasional telemarketer. *(Beat.)* Mom.

DUFF. I will not be mocked. I'm goin' over there! Oh! I'm goin'! I'm *so* goin' ... I'm there already!

(DUFF turns away to collect himself. He runs his hands through his unkempt hair. He straightens his over-shirt. Checks his breath in his palm. DUFF turns toward her, triumphant. He stops dead.)

TY. *(Without looking up from his crossword.)* Gone, isn't she.

(DUFF slumps back into his chair. He pokes at his fries. Pause.)

DUFF. You know what I really like, Ty?

TY. Breasts, Duff?

DUFF. Yeah.

(Blackout.)

END OF THE PLAY

Scheherazade

EMILY RODERER

Scheherazade

by
Emily Roderer

*premiered in January, 2000 at
Actors Theatre of Louisville*

Directed by Pascaline Bellegarde
Dramaturg: Laura Grace Pattillo

Cast

Man	Patrick Dall'Occhio
Girl	Shawna Anderson

Scenic Designer: Tom Burch
Lighting Designer: Andrew Vance
Costume Designer: Marcy Rector
Properties Designer: Tracey Rainey
Stage Manager: Nichole A. Shuman
Assistant Stage Manager: Juliane Taylor

Scheherazade

(The deck of a ship. Sounds of crowd, waves, ship fades in the background. a GIRL, sixteen, sits in a deckchair near a MAN. The MAN is writing in a ledger.)

GIRL. Are you a writer?

MAN. No.

GIRL. What are you doing?

MAN. Excuse me. Should you be talking to strangers?

GIRL. Strangers? We've been trapped on board with these people for almost two weeks. Don't you feel like you've known each and every one of them your whole life?

MAN. No.

GIRL. I do. And the rain! I've been trapped in a cabin with my aunt and my cousin for three days. I could jump overboard.

MAN. *(Continues writing.)* How dramatic.

GIRL. How do you keep from being bored?

MAN. *(Still writing.)* I work.

GIRL. *(Doesn't take the hint.)* What do you do?

MAN. I'm a banker.

GIRL. You loan people money?

MAN. Where is your aunt?

GIRL. I don't know and I don't care. *(The MAN is writing again.)* I hate work.

MAN. You have to earn your keep?

GIRL. I won't have to. I'm going to marry a rich man who will take care of me.

MAN. And if you don't?

GIRL. I'll be a writer. I'm very good at stories. I've imagined a story for nearly every person on deck. Would you like to hear one?

MAN. Do I have a choice?

GIRL. See the woman over there with the funny hat and the shoes that don't fit?

MAN. Yes.

GIRL. The man to her left with the spectacle is a rich suitor. She's been tempting him the whole trip. He wants her to marry him, but she doesn't love him. She's in love with the bald man with his back to us. I've seen her pass notes to him every day. They've been lovers for years. It's so obvious, you'd think the man with the spectacle would realize, but he's a fool, so he doesn't. She marries one of these rich old fools once every … five years. Slowly, she poisons them with arsenic. When the old man croaks she sends for her bald lover and meets him on a boat, like this one, bound for Asia or Europe or maybe South America. They travel for a while together. Reaping the benefits of their merciless endeavor. Then, en route back to the United States, they find another of these bumbling idiots, like the man with the spectacle, and the wicked cycle starts all over again.

MAN. And your reasoning?

GIRL. The man with the spectacle is obviously a fool. Have you spoken to him? The woman is obviously a temptress, that's why she wears those ridiculous hats and shoes that don't fit. And the bald man is obviously her lover because he's constantly at her disposal and she passes him notes night and day.

MAN. The bald man is a steward on this ship. He takes dinner orders. The woman is a wealthy heiress prone to wearing eccentric clothing, and the fool is a fool trying to convince her to invest in his business.

GIRL. How do you know that?

MAN. I've had dinner with them three times.

GIRL. But isn't my story more interesting?

MAN. Yes, but only because they are so boring. And your story isn't remotely believable.

GIRL. Why not?

MAN. Because that woman isn't remotely enticing, and she'd have to be to lure money away from rich old fools.

GIRL. Enticing? Is that what you have to be?

MAN. Yes.

GIRL. And if you're not?

MAN. Well, some people have to work to earn their keep.

GIRL. Some people have to tutor their cousins in art and history and read to their aunt and get her shawl whenever she asks, and if you do something she doesn't like you apologize and when she threatens to leave you at home on her next trip you cry and plead, because you know being left at home is worse than being with her?

MAN. Not such a bad job, is it.

GIRL. It might be, if that's all you could do.

MAN. I have to go to work every day and count money and sign loans or not sign loans and refuse people money that they may have needed but you couldn't in good conscience let them have. And maybe they needed it because a baby was on the way or their mother was ill or they couldn't find work. Those are not easy decisions.

GIRL. You do all that?

MAN. Sometimes.

GIRL. I would like to do that. I would give them the money, if they needed it.

MAN. That's why little girls don't work in banks.

GIRL. Little girl. *(She laughs.)* That's why they study art and visit Europe with their aunts and wear gloves to parties.

MAN. Yes. *(The GIRL is silent. He is content for a moment and returns to work.)* Sometimes, I give them the money.

GIRL. I knew you did.

MAN. I make them pay it back.

GIRL. Of course, so you can loan it to other people.

MAN. Yes, sometimes.

GIRL. I thought you had a kind face, an imaginative face. That's why I thought you were a writer. You looked as though you understood people.

MAN. Humph.

GIRL. Don't you ever imagine stories?

MAN. *(Laughs.)* My job in the bank is so much more interesting.

GIRL. Tell me a story.

MAN. I don't tell stories.

GIRL. Everyone tells stories.

MAN. Not me.

GIRL. Not ever?

MAN. No.

GIRL. Never to your son or daughter?

MAN. I don't have any children.

GIRL. Never to a niece or nephew?

MAN. I don't have any family.

GIRL. Never to a lover.

MAN. You're too young to be talking about lovers.

GIRL. No, I'm not. I have to know all about them to be a writer.

MAN. Well, then you're too young to be talking about them to me.

GIRL. Then, say something, anything.

MAN. *(He starts softly, as if he is telling a secret.)* The man and woman behind us. The two sketching. Don't look.

GIRL. Yes.

MAN. They're both world famous artists. They're married, but they're traveling together as brother and sister.

GIRL. Why?

MAN. Because they don't like to have attention drawn to themselves. They pick their subjects from ordinary people. If people knew they were famous artists, they would behave differently in front of them and none of their art would be real.

GIRL. How do you know?

MAN. I had dinner with them last night.

GIRL. And they told you all this?

MAN. I have an honest face. They thought they could trust me, and I believe they've already finished sketching me.

GIRL. Are you going to be in a painting?

MAN. Probably not, but I was a useful exercise in the human form, but you never know. They could choose anyone as the subject for their next masterpiece.

GIRL. Anyone?

MAN. Anyone.

GIRL. *(She becomes self-conscious.)* How would you know if they used you in a painting?

MAN. You wouldn't, unless you asked.

GIRL. I'm not going to ask.

MAN. Why not? What's the harm?

GIRL. I'm not going to ask because you're not telling the truth.

MAN. I wouldn't lie.

GIRL. But you would tell a story.

MAN. I don't tell stories.

GIRL. You'd never tell me to go over and ask them if I was to be in their next painting, if they were really artists.

MAN. *(Laughs.)* Then, you learned something about telling a story.

GIRL. I knew it was a story!

MAN. But you believed me until the end.

GIRL. I didn't.

MAN. The trick is not to make the story too outrageous or ridiculous.

GIRL. How do you know about stories, if you don't tell them?

MAN. I used to tell stories.

GIRL. When?

MAN. That was a very long time ago.

GIRL. Who did you tell stories to?

MAN. A woman I used to know.

GIRL. Your wife?

MAN. No.

GIRL. Your lover?

MAN. How old are you?

GIRL. Why?

MAN. You shouldn't be discussing people's lovers. Why don't you have another try?

GIRL. Was she your mistress?

MAN. I meant why don't you tell another story.

GIRL. I know what you meant. What kind?

MAN. Tell me one that I'll believe.

GIRL. That's an awful lot of pressure.

MAN. I have faith in you.

GIRL. Who would you like me to tell a story about?

MAN. Anyone?

GIRL. Anyone on deck.

MAN. You.

GIRL. Me? *(Pause.)* I'm sixteen. I'm traveling with my aunt and my cousin, Amy. We've been abroad for the summer. My aunt took us to Europe for a bit of "culture." In my aunt's view, the trip was a miserable failure. She hired a third-rate governess to tutor us in French and take us to museums. The governess ran off with our cook.

MAN. Was he handsome?

GIRL. No he was hideous. It wasn't romantic. She was a shrew. He had a bit of money saved. I heard them discussing it in the garden one night. That's the only reason she went off with him.

MAN. Not the least bit exciting.

GIRL. It was sad. She didn't love him. When she left she pulled me aside and said, "Learn how to fend for yourself. Work if you have to, but it's easier, if you find someone to do it for you."

MAN. Not very romantic.

GIRL. No, I'd never marry for money.

MAN. Humph.

GIRL. My aunt was forced to be chaperon. She has gout and couldn't keep up with us. Amy and I smoked our first cigarette in the gardens at Versailles. Does that shock you?

MAN. No.

GIRL. The gardens are lovely. My aunt's gout got the worst of her, and we had to stay penned in the hotel room. She tried to occupy us. Amy is eighteen, and my aunt had wealthy suitors visit almost every day. One was an Italian nobleman. He fell in love with me. He visited every day and passed me notes. The trip ended abruptly when my aunt discovered us. She was very angry.

MAN. Because you're too young.

GIRL. No, she doesn't care about me. I have no money. She doesn't want me to marry well. She doesn't want me to marry at all. She wants me to take care of her in her old age.

MAN. You've read too many romantic novels.

GIRL. It's all true.

MAN. I believed the first part. The second part is stolen.

GIRL. He's followed me on board. He's so in love with me he's following me back to America. He wants to elope. He's been watching us this whole time. See him? The handsome, dark man with the wide brim hat. He thinks he's inconspicuous. Don't stare. I only decided to speak with you because I saw him coming over, and I thought he might try to kiss me. We'd be discovered.

MAN. Now you're being outrageous.

GIRL. It's a good story.

MAN. Oh yes. Very good for you.

GIRL. You half-way believed me.

MAN. Until it became ridiculous.

GIRL. It was more exciting than your story.

MAN. Yes, but you believed me.

GIRL. Only for a moment.

MAN. Your story would have been more believable if the nobleman hadn't been rich.

GIRL. No?

MAN. Or maybe not a nobleman at all.

GIRL. No?

MAN. No, a commoner and your wealthy aunt threatened to cut

you off if you married him.

GIRL. That's not a very happy story.

MAN. No, but maybe closer to the truth.

GIRL. But what if her money was really mine, at least some of it. And what if I just couldn't get to it.

MAN. You'd be in a pinch.

GIRL. But what if there was someone to help me?

MAN. You have a fine imagination.

GIRL. And what if that person was the man who controlled that money and all he had to do was help me just a little.

MAN. If only things were so simple.

GIRL. Did you tell the woman stories?

MAN. Oh yes.

GIRL. Were they believable?

MAN. They were hopeful.

GIRL. What happened to her?

MAN. Let's just say she had an aunt who didn't approve.

GIRL. What if someone could have helped her?

MAN. I would have been very happy.

GIRL. And you would have paid every penny back?

MAN. Yes.

GIRL. I believe you.

END OF THE PLAY

House of Cards

RICHARD KELLER

House of Cards

by
Richard Keller

*premiered in April, 2003 at
Actors Theatre of Louisville*

Directed by Steve Moulds
Dramaturg: Susannah Engstrom

Cast

Warren	Jason Kaminsky
Delia	Jen Grigg
Staci	Lori McNally
Jack	Brian Nemiroff

Scenic Designer: Brenda Ellis
Costume Designer: Andrea Scott
Lighting Designer: Sandy Harned
Sound Designer: Ben Marcum
Properties Designers: Tracey Rainey and Ann Marie Werner
Stage Manager: Abigail Wright
Assistant Stage Manager: Denise Olivieri

CHARACTERS

WARREN: late twenties-early thirties
DELIA: late twenties-early thirties
STACI: late twenties-early thirties
JACK: late twenties-early thirties

SETTING

Warren and Delia's apartment.
The time is the present.

House of Cards

(Scene: Warren and Delia's living room. WARREN is counting poker chips, setting up for a game. DELIA is wiping the table.)

WARREN. What's his name again?

DELIA. I told you his name. Don't act like it's difficult to remember his name. Like he's new to your game so it's a big hassle to say his name.

WARREN. I just wish you would've spoken to me first. You don't spring this on me. This here is my thing. There might not be room at the table for one more. And, point of fact, these are my friends, not yours.

DELIA. Staci's my friend.

WARREN. Staci lives in the building.

DELIA. So?

WARREN. So she's joint property. *(Counts another stack of chips.)* Where you going?

DELIA. What?

WARREN. While we're playing.

DELIA. The bedroom. *(WARREN looks at her.)* You won't even know I'm here. *(Pause.)* The movies. I'm going to the movies. And then I'm going to a sports bar, pick up the man with the least amount of hair loss, ride him like a mechanical bull, and I'll be back before dawn.

WARREN. You're going to wait until whatshisname gets here, right?

DELIA. Look, he's new at the office. He's a bit shy but very, I repeat very, nice. You'll like him. Okay? *(Doorbell rings.)* I said you'll like him.

WARREN. Yeah, I'll like him. Christ, it ain't a date.

DELIA. He's a hell of a lot nicer than Staci.

(DELIA answers the door. STACI enters carrying a six-pack. She wears latex gloves.)

STACI. Who's a hell of a lot nicer than me?

WARREN. *(To DELIA.)* I told you your voice carries.

DELIA. Can you hear us in your apartment?

STACI. No. Sometimes.

WARREN. See that.

DELIA. When we're ....

STACI. No. Sometimes.

DELIA. I was talking about my cousin Stacey.

WARREN. She was talking about you.

STACI. I sort of figured.

WARREN. What's with the latex gloves?

STACI. I was opening my mail. So who's nicer than me?

DELIA. Jack. His name is Jack. He's going to join you tonight.

WARREN. Stace, you think you need to worry?

STACI. Why? Am I out of the game? Is Jack replacing me?

WARREN. The gloves. They seem to be targeting people with higher profiles.

DELIA. You know, like people who work.

STACI. Copycat mailings. I get a lot of direct marketing shit. Franklin Mint. Bank of Delaware. I'm suspicious. Hey, are you trying to set me up with Jack?

DELIA. No.

STACI. I mean, that's cool. I might've worn something different is all. I bought boot-cut jeans.

(Doorbell rings.)

DELIA. He's here to play poker. Doesn't even know you exist.

STACI. Yeeeoooow!

(WARREN and STACI snicker. DELIA goes to the door.)

DELIA. Remember ....

WARREN. He's very, very nice.

(The doorbell rings again. DELIA opens the door. It's JACK. He is dressed like the one-eyed jack from the deck of cards. He wears

*an eye patch, a trifold hat, and a multicolored, thigh-length
smock with many bright red hearts embroidered on it, including a
large one on the front. He has on a pair of blue jeans. His mustache is trimmed and curled at the ends. He carries a six-pack of
beer. DELIA is speechless. JACK steps into the apartment.)*

JACK. Hey, Delia. Where should I put these?

DELIA. What ... uh ... what is this?

JACK. Lighthouse Lager. It's a microbrew. It's cold. You must
be Warren.

(Shakes WARREN's hand.)

WARREN. Yeah ... and ... you must be Jack.

JACK. Staci?

STACI. You know my name?

JACK. Yeah, well, Delia has mentioned you.

STACI. Oh, she did?

DELIA. Uh, Jack ....

JACK. Delia.

DELIA. What ... what are you, um ... you're all "decked" out.

JACK. Good one. Nice.

DELIA. I'm a bit taken aback.

STACI. Be grateful he's not the suicide king.

WARREN. I dig that eye patch, man. Hathaway shirts. Moshe
Dayan. Cool.

DELIA. Did you think it was a costume party?

JACK. No, I, uh ... you know ... it's the weekend ... and my name
is Jack. I ... just thought I'd ... is this inappropriate?

DELIA. The guys usually don't dress up for poker.

WARREN. Whatever. As long as you brought along some coin.
I'll take one of those Lighthouse Lagers.

JACK. Oh, you'll like those. Just a hint of stone-ground wheat in
there.

STACI. I see you're wearing your heart on your sleeve.

JACK. Among other places.

(They share a laugh.)

WARREN. I always wanted to wear an eye patch.

JACK. Me too. And finally I just said screw it. I'm wearing an eye patch.

STACI. *(Aside to DELIA.)* You weren't fixing us up, but he just happens to know my name.

DELIA. My God, he's a freak.

STACI. Yeah. *(Pause.)* I like him.

DELIA. Warren is never going to let me hear the end of this.

JACK. You going to play tonight, Delia?

DELIA. No, no, I never play. This is Warren's night in with the boys. And Staci. Sacred. It's sacred. I'm off to the movies, and I don't ... I don't play poker. I'm not good at games.

JACK. I think the lady doth protest too much.

DELIA. You what?

JACK. Oh, that's ... I came up with this way of talking. For the one-eyed jack persona. Sort of ... "methinks that I doth to ... la-la-la." You know, sort of ... very flowery. Shakespearean almost.

DELIA. You're an actuary at an insurance company.

JACK. No, I'm the jack of hearts. *(Again, JACK and STACI laugh together.)* Why don't we play a few practice hands until everyone gets here? What do you say, Warren?

WARREN. No harm in that I guess.

DELIA. I find it disturbing that he's dressed like a playing card.

WARREN. Jeez! Company at twelve o'clock.

STACI. *(To JACK.)* She gets bent out of shape on poker nights. When I walked in she told me that you're a hell of a lot nicer than me.

JACK. Wow. That's not the Delia I know from the office.

STACI. So Delia tells me you're an actuary.

DELIA. I didn't tell you that.

STACI. Yeah, but I overheard you say it to the jack of hearts. *(To JACK.)* So, how very exciting.

JACK. You know, I'm, uh ... I'm feeling a little uncomfortable. Like this wasn't a good idea.

WARREN. No, no. C'mon now.

JACK. No, I feel like I owe Delia an apology.

WARREN. Please. We're just all a little ... what ....

STACI. Tense.

WARREN. Yeah, a little tense.

JACK. Delia ... I'm sorry ...

WARREN. Delia ....

DELIA. No, Jack it's not you. It's me. You took me by surprise.

It's ... we're fine. I'm fine. Are you fine?
    JACK. Yeah, I'm ... fine.
    DELIA. Are you guys fine? Staci, are you mad at me?
    STACI. Yeah, somewhat, but I'm fine. Let's play some cards.

(They sit at the table.)

    WARREN. Don't ante up. This is practice. *(WARREN hands the deck of cards to JACK.)* Be my guest.

(JACK shuffles. And then shuffles some more. And then keeps on shuffling. It becomes awkward, then really awkward. And then in a slightly southern, wholesome voice, JACK recites from memory.)

    JACK. "When I count the number of spots on the deck of cards, I find 365, the number of days in a year. There's 52 cards, the number of weeks in a year. There's 4 suits, the number of weeks in a month. There's 12 picture cards, the number of months in a year. There's 13 tricks, the number of weeks in a quarter. So you see, Sir, my pack of cards serves me as a Bible, almanac, and prayer book."

(Pause.)

    DELIA. See, now that was sort of weird.
    STACI. Yeah.
    WARREN. *(Overlapping.)* Yup.
    JACK. *(Overlapping.)* Yeah. *(Pause.)* Wink Martindale's "Deck of Cards." *(Shuffles some more and some more.)* When I was growing up, my parents would host Bible study in our home. Once a month maybe. Nothing too ... zealous. I wasn't into it. I was sort of embarrassed by it. But that song. I just thought that song was so cool 'cause this guy was finding the meaning of God or life somewhere other than the usual places. Like he could read meaning into the numbers on the cards. *(Long pause, places the deck down.)* I don't know how to play poker. *(Pause.)* We're creating new actuary tables at the office. Determining a set of risk factors depending on where people work. Calculating life expectancies. What ifs.... What if you work in an office tower. What if the office tower is over twenty stories. What if the office tower is over fifty stories. What if a famous person works in the building. What if you open the mail of the famous person that works

in the tower over fifty stories. What if you open the mail of the famous person that works in the twenty-story office tower. How famous
can a person be if they only work in a twenty-story office tower. How
will it impact insurance rates. What kind of premiums will be paid
out. *(Pause.)* I just moved here a couple of months ago. I don't know
anyone. If something happened to me right now, nobody would know
to look for me. Or no, a few would, if they cared to. If I didn't show
up for work. *(Pause.)* I wanted to be the jack of hearts. The lover. The
soldier of fortune. I wanted to wear an eye patch.

(Pause.)

    STACI. I bought boot-cut jeans. We're all frightened.

(Long pause, doorbell rings.)

    JACK. You know what? I, uh ... yeah. I'm going to head back
downtown.
    WARREN. No. No. Definitely not. Stay. You're staying. We'd
like you to stay. I'm going to teach you how to play poker. And
Delia's going to stay too. Right, Delia? You want to throw back some
Lighthouse Lagers? It's got like wheat in it or something. Right? You
don't mind missing the movie? You want to stay. Right, Del? Will
you please stay?
    DELIA. Yeah, I'll stay.
    JACK. You sure?
    DELIA. Yeah.
    WARREN. What do you say, Jack?
    JACK. I'd like that.
    WARREN. Okay! The gang's all here. *(Doorbell rings.)* Stace.
Get the door. *(She goes to the door.)* Let the games begin.

*(STACI hesitates for a moment, removes her gloves, and then opens
    the door to their friends' hurrahs.)*

END OF THE PLAY

The Office

KATE HOFFOWER

For Robin, Jeanette & Jillian

The Office

by
Kate Hoffower

*premiered in January, 2001 at
Actors Theatre of Louisville*

Directed by Pascaline Bellgarde
Dramaturg: Tanya Palmer

Cast

One	Jessica Browne-White
Two	Shoshona Currier
Three	Emera Felice Krauss

Scenic Designer: Brenda Ellis
Costume Designer: Marcy Rector
Lighting Designer: Andrew Vance
Sound Designer: Kate Ducey
Stage Manager: Erin Tatge
Assistant Stage Manager: Sarah Hodges

The Office was first produced in a staged reading at
Chicago Dramatist's Workshop

CHARACTERS

ONE
TWO
THREE

TIME

The present.

The Office

(Lights up as an unassuming customer service representative enters [THREE]. She is normal-looking, on the bland side. She takes a seat at the upstage center desk and begins to shuffle papers. She does not speak, but works quietly at her desk throughout the play. She is rarely acknowledged by ONE and TWO but observes them carefully.)

ONE. I'm bored.
TWO. Me too.
ONE. I've never been this bored.
TWO. Me neither.
ONE. Never in my entire life.
TWO. Never. Not this bored.
ONE. I'm beyond bored.
TWO. I'm *beyond* being bored.
ONE. I'm beyond *being* beyond—
TWO. bored.
ONE. I'm—
TWO. so bored.
ONE. So very, very, very—
TWO. bored.
ONE and TWO. I
ONE and TWO. am
ONE and TWO. so
ONE and TWO. *bored.*
ONE. *(Stuffing a pencil in her ear.)* What time is it?
TWO. *(Stuffing a pencil in her ear.)* Nine a.m.
ONE. *(Stuffing a pencil in her nose.)* What time is it now?
TWO. *(Stuffing a pencil in her nose.)* Nine a.m. and three seconds.

ONE. *(Stuffing her remaining nasal and aural orifices with pencils.)* Now?

TWO. *(Likewise.)* Nine a.m. and three of the most boring seconds I have ever experienced in my *life.*

ONE. Never

TWO. ever

ONE. have

TWO. I

ONE. ever

TWO. been

ONE. this

ONE and TWO. BORED!

ONE. If I have pretzels on my desk today, and he comes by and eats them again without asking, I'm going to punch him.

TWO. Tell him that's all you can afford to bring for lunch on the miserable salary he pays you, and if he doesn't keep his hands *off,* you'll have him arrested.

ONE. If he fires me how much can I collect in unemployment?

TWO. Probably more than you're making now. Hey—have you ever noticed that sometimes when he's standing over your desk talking at you that he sort of reaches down and smoothes the front of his pants ... *excessively?*

ONE. Yes! But it's more like he's patting himself—trying to calm himself down.

TWO. It seems pretty sick to me.

ONE. Maybe it's just a habit.

TWO. Yeah. Maybe when he was a kid his parents wouldn't let him have a pet. So instead of a dog or a cat—

ONE. he stared petting *himself!*

ONE and TWO. Aghhhh!!!!!!

TWO. If only he wasn't looking over my shoulder constantly—if he was just here part-time it wouldn't be so bad.

ONE. Yeah, well, good luck. He already works like two-hundred hours a week.

TWO. He'd have to cut down if he had a heart attack.

ONE. Great. I'll sneak up behind him and yell boo.

TWO. No. I'm serious. Think about it. The average person burns about two-thousand calories a day. And you have to eat thirty-five-hundred calories more than you burn in order to gain a pound. He's fairly sedentary, and he doesn't workout or anything.—And I know he easily eats at least two-thousand calories a day already. So if we could just get him to eat a little more and gain what? About fifty pounds? Would that do it?

ONE. I don't know. It would help I guess.

TWO. OK. So how long would it take him to gain that much?

ONE. *(Hesitantly.)* Well, thirty-five-hundred calories times fifty pounds is ... *(She uses her calculator.)* a hundred-seventy-five-thousand extra calories. If he ate—let's say an extra five-hundred calories a day—that's like two extra candy bars—it would take ....

TWO. A hundred-seventy-five-thousand calories?

ONE. Yeah.

TWO. OK. A hundred-seventy-five-thousand calories divided by five-hundred is—

ONE. three hundred and fifty days.

TWO. Almost a year. But maybe it would take less than fifty pounds if we could add more stress to his life.

ONE. Yeah ... but how would we get him to eat the extra two candy bars a day in the first place?

TWO. It wouldn't have to be candy bars. I could bring in donuts every once in awhile. You could bring in cookies now and then. — And there's always holiday food!

ONE. But what if it works? What if we kill him and get arrested for murder?

TWO. We couldn't get arrested. We didn't *make* him eat it. Besides, he'll probably just have a mild heart attack and have to cut down his work week. That would be perfect.

ONE. I guess so. *(Changing the subject.)* So whadja watch last night?

TWO. Sunday movie. You?

ONE. I went to bed early.

TWO. You always go to bed early.

ONE. You always go home and watch TV.

TWO. No. Sometimes I go home and watch TV and read *People Magazine* and eat ice cream. —All at the same time.

(Pause.)

ONE. Jesus! Why are we still *here?*

TWO. I don't know.

ONE. I can remember being twelve years old and having my life completely planned out. I was going to graduate from the Eastman School of Music, sing professionally until I was twenty-six, get married, have two children, and then work part-time—*if* I felt like it.

TWO. Yikes!

ONE. Well, *you* can't have dreamt of a career in customer service.

TWO. No.

ONE. No.

(Pause.)

TWO. I was going to be a brain surgeon.

(THREE laughs. ONE and TWO both turn to look at her. THREE quickly returns to work.)

ONE. A *brain* surgeon?

TWO. Yes! I remember watching cartoons one Saturday morning and seeing this commercial for some doll, and all these little girls in pink dresses were sitting around, very well-behaved, brushing its hair, practically melting with sweetness. And the next ad was a bunch of boys skating through a fantasy world of castles and dragons, yelling and screaming and having the time of their lives. And then the very next ad was for that same stupid pink doll! So I told my mom about it and she said "That's because girls are supposed to sit at home and have babies, and boys are supposed to go out and have a whole hell of a lot of fun and not worry about anything." So I said "Well I don't want to sit around and have babies. I want to have fun too." And she said "Great. Be a brain surgeon."

ONE. She said "Great, be a brain surgeon?"

TWO. She said "Great. Be a brain surgeon."

ONE. And?

TWO. And I took her seriously. I went to the library and started researching the brain. But then I started have trouble with math and science. I practically failed high school. And I eventually gave up med school dreams for art…. I've done some fantastic pastels of the temporal lobe.

ONE. My dad called me last night. It really scared me because he never calls, so I figured something must be wrong. I couldn't believe it was him. He said "Are you OK?" And I said "I'm fine, why?" and he said "I just got a feeling that something was wrong and I wanted to call." And suddenly I thought—Yes Dad. Something *is* wrong. I want to be a singer. I've dreamt about it my entire life but somehow I've ended up here. I work for seven-fifty an hour. I file, I answer phones, and I photocopy, eight and a half hours a day, forty-two and a half hours a week, and every minute of every day my soul rots away just a little bit more. I'm twenty-eight years old and I'm dying. I'm already dead. I might as well be. I wanted to say "Make me seven years old again Daddy. Stand with me on the top of the diving board and hold my hand as I look a million miles down at the long black arrows on the bottom of the pool. Then squeeze my hand and tell me that everything is going to be OK. We're just going to count to three and jump."

(Pause.)

TWO. Take your bra off.

ONE. What!?

TWO. I dare you to take your bra off and wear it outside your clothes.

ONE. No! Why?

TWO. It will be a break from the monotony of our otherwise tedious and meaningless lives.

ONE. No!

TWO. I'll let you have the good stapler.

ONE. No.

TWO. I'll change the fax paper for you from now on.

ONE. *No.*

TWO. I'll teach you how to use Quark.

ONE. No....

TWO. Quark Xpress, the new version. I'll teach you how to set tabs, create master guides, and kern. You will learn how to make entries into the auxiliary dictionary, how to start modifying, and how to establish a baseline grid.

ONE. Will you teach me how to use the horizontal/vertical scale?

TWO. Yes!

ONE. OK, OK. I'll do it. But *you* have to do it too.

TWO. Why?

ONE. Because if you do, I'll agree to the heart attack thing. I'll start my part tomorrow by bringing in two dozen double chocolate donuts.

TWO. His favorite!

ONE. Exactly.

TWO. OK. Deal.

ONE. All right then. On your mark—

TWO. Get set—

ONE. Go! *(They both take off their bras underneath their shirts and re-hook them on top. There can be some ad-libbing, ouches and laughter. THREE watches for a moment then silently joins them. They do not notice her. THREE sits back down at her desk and resumes work while ONE and TWO finish.)* He's going to be here any minute.

TWO. He probably won't even notice!

ONE. He'll probably take one look and start rubbing himself like crazy.

ONE and TWO. Aggghhhh!!!!!!

(They laugh again and return to their desks. Pause. They begin looking for something to do.)

ONE. I am really bored.

TWO. Really, really bored.

ONE. Really

TWO. really

ONE. really

TWO. bored.

(Lights fade to black.)

END OF PLAY

Paper Thin

LINDSAY PRICE

Paper Thin

by
Lindsay Price

premiered in January, 2001 at
Actors Theatre of Louisville

Directed by Pascaline Bellgarde
Dramaturg: Steve Moulds

Cast

Sweetie	Andrew Jackson
Punkin	Misty Dawn Jordan
Man	Breton Nicholson
Woman	Maesie Speer

Scenic Designer: Brenda Ellis
Costume Designer: Karen Hall
Lighting Designer: Andrew Vance
Properties Designer: Doc Manning
Stage Manager: Erin Tatge
Assistant Stage Manager: Sarah Hodges
Fight Director: Brent Langdon

CHARACTERS

SWEETIE: Male, late 20's/early 30's
PUNKIN: Female, late 20's/early 30's
TWO OFFSTAGE VOICES: One male
and one female *(can be live or on tape.)*

SETTING

A living room.
The play takes place today.

Paper Thin

(The scene is a living room. This should be simply represented by a wall [flat] with a couch and a coffee table in front of the flat. The setting represents the living space of an upwardly mobile, two-income, childless household.
A man [SWEETIE] is onstage putting the finishing touches to what looks like a romantic evening at home. There is mood music, candlelight, appetizers and glasses on the coffee table. There is also a pad and pencil on the coffee table. He is in the middle of opening the champagne bottle which he places on ice. He hears keys jingling and the front door opening. In a scurry, SWEETIE looks for something to throw over the champagne—he uses his jacket. We hear the voice of a woman [PUNKIN] offstage.)

PUNKIN. *(Offstage.)* Hello!
SWEETIE. Don't move Punkin! Stay right where you are.
PUNKIN. *(Offstage.)* Why?
SWEETIE. Stay there!

(He rushes offstage.)

PUNKIN. *(Offstage.)* Sweetie, I'm really tired....
SWEETIE. *(Offstage.)* Close your eyes.
PUNKIN. *(Offstage.)* It's been a horrendous day.
SWEETIE. *(Offstage.)* Close them. Now walk.
PUNKIN. Sweetie....
SWEETIE. Left, right, left, right.

(SWEETIE leads PUNKIN into the room. PUNKIN has one hand over her eyes, the other is holding an expensive-looking briefcase. PUNKIN is very well dressed in a suit, so is SWEETIE for that

matter.)

PUNKIN. *(Talking as she walks, still with hand over eyes.)* The Rankin deal went right in the toilet this afternoon. And they are redoing the seventeenth floor so the power cut out three times, and all three times were....

SWEETIE. And stop.

PUNKIN. This isn't very special is it? I am so not in the mood.

SWEETIE. Open your eyes. Wait! Give me your briefcase. Ok, open your eyes.

(She does so, taking in the room with wide eyes. She picks up the pad.)

PUNKIN. No.

SWEETIE. Yes.

PUNKIN. No!

SWEETIE. Surprise!

PUNKIN. But it's Tuesday!

SWEETIE. Are you in the mood now, Punkin?

PUNKIN. This is exactly what I'm in the mood for! So when is it? Is he home yet? Do I have time to change?

SWEETIE. There's plenty of time.

PUNKIN. How do you know?

SWEETIE. We had a long chat in the elevator this morning. Are you ready?

PUNKIN. Lay it on me.

SWEETIE. First of all, he has a dinner meeting tonight.

PUNKIN. So he'll be drinking. On a Tuesday!

SWEETIE. And she has been banging pots around for about an hour now.

PUNKIN. Did she know about the dinner meeting?

SWEETIE. I don't think so.

PUNKIN. Crossed lines of communication. I love it!

SWEETIE. And....

(With a flourish, he reveals the champagne.)

PUNKIN. Champagne? What for?

SWEETIE. He also told me that today is their wedding anniversary. I thought we'd do a little celebrating ourselves.

PUNKIN. *(Jumping up and down like an excited schoolgirl.)* I can't believe it! He has a dinner meeting on their anniversary! She's been cooking for over an hour! This is so great! I'm going to go change. Call me if it starts.

(PUNKIN dashes off. SWEETIE pours two glasses of champagne, singing to himself. PUNKIN calls from offstage.)

PUNKIN. *(Offstage.)* Hey Sweetie....
SWEETIE. Yes.

(PUNKIN comes on in the middle of changing.)

PUNKIN. Did you know about this when I called you about the dry-cleaning?
SWEETIE. Yes.
PUNKIN. And when you called me about next weekend?
SWEETIE. Yes.
PUNKIN. You dirty dog! You didn't let on for a second.

(She exits again to continue changing.)

SWEETIE. I wanted to surprise you. I left work early so I could swing by Henri's.
PUNKIN. *(Offstage.)* You went to Henri's? This is going to be fabulous!
SWEETIE. Punkin?
PUNKIN. Uh huh?
SWEETIE. I want him this time.
PUNKIN. *(Entering dressed in sweats.)* I wanted him!
SWEETIE. You always want him, and might I add, you always get him.
PUNKIN. He's more fun. She is so repetitive.
SWEETIE. Just this once. Please?
PUNKIN. Well, since you went to all this trouble. On a Tuesday … he's yours.

(SWEETIE grabs PUNKIN playfully and gives her a hug and a smooch.)

SWEETIE. Now, have a seat, drink some champagne, and eat. I'll be right back.

(SWEETIE exits. PUNKIN sits on the couch and takes a glass of champagne and picks through the food.)

PUNKIN. *(Taking a sip of champagne.)* Ahhhh. That hits the spot. I can't believe they've been married a whole year. I'm surprised it's lasted so long. And you know it's only our good will that doesn't get them thrown out of the building. When it was just Saturdays, that was bearable, you just stick your head between two pillows for twenty minutes. But then it was Friday, Saturday, Sunday, and now Tuesday, who knows where it will end. I mean … ooooh these crab puffs are so delicious! It's a good thing you came up with this idea. It puts a fresh perspective on the whole situation. *(SWEETIE enters; he too is wearing sweats. He sits on the couch.)* Have a crab puff, Sweetie. Henri outdid himself.

SWEETIE. *(As he sits he grabs a crab puff.)* Ahhh. I love these guilty pleasures. Did you try the baby quiches?

PUNKIN. *(Her mouth full.)* Ummm Hmmmm.

(They share a moment of chewing.)

SWEETIE. Do you ever feel … you know … guilty?

PUNKIN. About this? Maybe a little. At first. But it's the perfect solution. This way, they can do what they do and we can have some fun. Don't you think?

SWEETIE. *(Raising his champagne glass.)* To fun.

PUNKIN. *(Raising her glass.)* To fun. *(They clink glasses. A door is heard slamming offstage.)* Is that him? Get the pad!

(SWEETIE grabs the pad and pencil from the coffee table. PUNKIN glues her ear to the wall.)

SWEETIE. What's happening?

PUNKIN. Nothing yet. He hasn't even said hello to her.

PUNKIN. Did he get her an anniversary present?

SWEETIE. He said he was going to try and remember to pick one up on the way home.

PUNKIN. She starts it.

SWEETIE. I'll bet he's been fuming all day—they had to go to her mother's for dinner last night.

PUNKIN. This is totally unfair! You get insider information.

SWEETIE. Despite which, you always win.

PUNKIN. True. *(She hears something.)* Shh. Shh.

(The conversation on the other side of the wall becomes clearer. The voices are harsh, contrasting with the bubbly voices of SWEETIE and PUNKIN. The fight should not be exaggerated or funny. NOTE: These voices can either be live behind the wall or taped. SWEETIE and PUNKIN don't necessarily have to wait for the MALE or FEMALE to stop talking to deliver their lines.)

MALE. I told you I had a dinner meeting!

FEMALE. No you didn't. I've been cooking for over an hour.

MALE. That's not my fault. I told you about the meeting.

SWEETIE. One for me!

(He marks a point on the pad.)

FEMALE. When did you tell me? When?

PUNKIN. Did he tell her?

MALE. I told you three times yesterday.

SWEETIE. He's bluffing.

FEMALE. You hardly spoke to me yesterday. I think I would remember if you mentioned a dinner meeting.

MALE. I told you! It's not my fault that you forgot.

PUNKIN. I get a point!

SWEETIE. For what?

PUNKIN. He said "It's not my fault" twice. No repeats!

FEMALE. What am I supposed to do with all this food?

MALE. I don't care what you do with it for Christ's sake.

SWEETIE. Who brings up the anniversary?

FEMALE. Don't you walk away from me!

PUNKIN. Do you have to ask?

MALE. What, what is it?

FEMALE. Did you forget what today is?

PUNKIN. Point!

MALE. Look, I had a hard day. I want to sit and watch TV. Is that too much to ask?

SWEETIE. He's backing off.

PUNKIN. She's on a role!

SWEETIE. Come on man, don't do this to me. Get in the fight!

FEMALE. You did, you forgot.

PUNKIN. You give it to him!

MALE. I didn't forget.

FEMALE. You forgot our anniversary. You forgot the one day that is supposed to mean something in our marriage!

MALE. *(Coming overtop.)* Mean something! There is nothing in this marriage that means something to me!

PUNKIN. Ooooooh, that's a low blow.

SWEETIE. Point!

FEMALE. What is that supposed to mean?

MALE. You want me to spell it out? Ok. This chair means nothing. *(There is the sound of a chair overturning.)* This food means nothing. *(There is the sound of dishes crashing to the floor.)*

PUNKIN. Is he wrecking the place?

SWEETIE. How many points for that?

FEMALE. Stop it! Stop it!

MALE. This table means nothing. *(There is the sound of a table turning over.)*

FEMALE. Stop it! What the hell are you doing!

MALE. You want me to go on? You want me to?

FEMALE. I hate you! I wish I never married you!

MALE. You shut up!

FEMALE. I hate you I hate you

MALE. Shut up!

FEMALE. I HATE YOU I HATE YOU I

MALE. SHUT UP SHUT UP SHUT UP!!!

(There is the sound of a slap. And another. And another. There is the sound of a FEMALE crying out. There is the sound of heavy feet walking away, kicking furniture and broken dishes. A door opens and slams shut. There is the sound of a FEMALE quietly crying. SWEETIE and PUNKIN are frozen in shock.)

PUNKIN. He hit her.

SWEETIE. He's never done that before.

PUNKIN. He hit her. *(She puts her ear to the wall.)* I don't believe it. He hit her.

SWEETIE. What's she doing?

PUNKIN. Crying. She's not supposed to do that. She's supposed to stand up to him. She was winning. I was winning with her, for the first time. She ....

(PUNKIN backs away from the wall. She goes to the phone and picks it up.)

SWEETIE. What are you doing?

PUNKIN. Calling the police.

SWEETIE. Why?

PUNKIN. He hit her, three times. I'm not going to let him get away with that.

SWEETIE. We don't know what happened.

PUNKIN. I heard slaps.

SWEETIE. We think they were slaps.

PUNKIN. He wrecked the apartment!

SWEETIE. We shouldn't interfere.

PUNKIN. They are our neighbors.

SWEETIE. It's none of our business. He probably won't do it again.

PUNKIN. How do you know?

(She starts to dial the phone. SWEETIE takes it from her.)

SWEETIE. I think we should stay out of it.

PUNKIN. Give that back!

SWEETIE. What happens if they resent us for getting involved? What if they don't want anyone to know? I have to see this guy every morning on the elevator, can you imagine what that's going to be like after we call the cops on him? I have to associate with him.

PUNKIN. And I guess it doesn't matter that she's cleaning up a trashed kitchen and nursing a black eye.

SWEETIE. We don't know she has a black eye.

PUNKIN. Why don't we call the police and not leave our names?

SWEETIE. Who else would it be, Punkin?

PUNKIN. Don't call me that.

SWEETIE. We're the only apartment that shares a wall with them. Who else would it be?

PUNKIN. So we do nothing.

SWEETIE. Why don't we wait a week? Ok? It was their anniversary. He had a bad day, he was drinking. That's a lot of stressors. We shouldn't jump to conclusions that we can't prove. Put the phone down. If it happens again, we call. I'll dial the number myself. Ok? Ok? Michelle?

PUNKIN. Ok.

(She slowly puts the phone on the coffee table.)

SWEETIE. Now. Would you like some more champagne?

PUNKIN. Please.

(AS SWEETIE reaches away from PUNKIN to get the champagne, PUNKIN leaps off the couch and takes the phone with her.)

SWEETIE. What are you doing?

PUNKIN. I don't want to wait a week.

SWEETIE. You are not calling the police.

PUNKIN. And you're going to stop me?

SWEETIE. If I have to.

PUNKIN. Are you going to hold me down? Maybe you'll knock the phone out of my hands? I know, you'll knock me down! That should do it.

SWEETIE. You are such a hypocrite.

PUNKIN. I'm a what?

SWEETIE. You like it when he yells at her.

PUNKIN. I what?

SWEETIE. You win the game! You want him to yell as loud as he can! You push and push....

PUNKIN. This is completely different.

SWEETIE. A scream is this far away from a push. You've been egging him on.

PUNKIN. How dare you say that. How dare you! Like you are any better than I am. You came up with this stupid game in the first place! You're the one who suggested we listen in, you're the one who's been egging them on.

SWEETIE. You're the one who gets excited. Give it to her! Give it to her!

PUNKIN. Shut up.

SWEETIE. Come on, go after her!

PUNKIN. Shut up!
SWEETIE. Come on, stand up to her!
PUNKIN. You're just as bad! Just as bad!
SWEETIE. IT'S ALL YOUR FAULT!

(PUNKIN slaps SWEETIE across the face. SWEETIE slaps PUNKIN across the face. PUNKIN drops the phone. The two of them pounce on it. They each get an end and it looks to be a fight to the death.

A door opens and slams. The neighbor is back. SWEETIE and PUNKIN are frozen, each still holding onto the phone. They hear the murmured conversation coming from next door. It sounds like reconciliation, but the dialogue is muffled.

SWEETIE and PUNKIN move closer to the wall, straining to hear what's being said. They both plant their ears to the wall.)

MALE. I'm sorry, I'm so sorry, It won't happen again. I love you.
FEMALE. I love you too. I love you too. I'm sorry. I'm so sorry.

(MALE and FEMALE repeat this indefinitely as the lights fade to black.)

END OF THE PLAY

Salesgirl

STEPHEN LEVI

Salesgirl

by
Stephen Levi

premiered in April, 2003 at
Actors Theatre of Louisville

Directed by Erica Bradshaw
Dramaturg: Susannah Engstrom

Cast

Cindy McPherson	Natalie Sander
Marvin Chomsky	Richard Furlong

Scenic Designer: Brenda Ellis
Costume Designer: Andrea Scott
Lighting Designer: Sandy Harned
Sound Designer: Ben Marcum
Properties Designers: Tracey Rainey and Ann Marie Werner
Stage Manager: Abigail Wright
Assistant Stage Manager: Denise Olivieri

CHARACTERS

CINDY MCPHERSON
MARVIN CHOMSKY

TIME AND PLACE

The toy department of Marshall Field's Department Store in Chicago.
Christmas Eve. 1947.

Salesgirl

(It is Christmas Eve, 1947—in Marshall Field's toy department, Chicago. The floor is littered with toys, crumpled gift-wrap and crushed boxes. A giant, gift bag display—tall as a person— becomes a convenient receptacle for CINDY McPHERSON to toss trash into. Holiday music is piped in.

At rise, CINDY tidies up, puts toys away, clears debris. Exhausted, she sits, surreptitiously looks about, removes shoes, rubs feet— huge sigh of relief. MARVIN CHOMSKY enters pulling toy-filled red wagon, topped by cymbal-clapping mechanical monkey. He spots CINDY. She quickly puts shoes on, resumes cleanup. Closing out the cash register, MARVIN, smitten, can't keep his eyes off her loveliness.)

MARVIN. *(Flat mid-western accent.)* Well, Cindy, the end of another terrific holiday sales season. *(Too tired to talk, CINDY smiles faintly. They put items away before MARVIN speaks again.)* Tomorrow and Sunday off.

CINDY. *(Grateful sigh.)* Christmas day—church.

(Silence.)

MARVIN. Monday ....
CINDY. *(Moans.)* Returns.

(Silence.)

MARVIN. Tuesday ....
CINDY. More returns.
MARVIN. Wednesday ....
CINDY. *Big* sales day. *More* returns. *More* exhaustion.

193

MARVIN. And maybe marriage.

CINDY. Marriage?! Somebody's getting married?!

MARVIN. *(Presents ring box.)* If a certain salesgirl says I do to a certain floor manager of a certain toy department in the heart of downtown Chicago.

CINDY. *(Opens box, shocked.)* Marvin!

MARVIN. It's a diamond.

CINDY. I can see it is. Is it real?!

MARVIN. You've never seen a real diamond before?

CINDY. Not this close to my naked finger.

MARVIN. It's an engagement ring.

CINDY. No kidding. How many carats?

MARVIN. I forgot to ask. I just saw it. I liked it. I bought it.

CINDY. Did you get it here in the store?

MARVIN. Where else?

CINDY. *(Squints, reads inside inscription.)* It's a Marshall Field's ring?! Our own brand?!

MARVIN. *(Beams.)* Only the best.

CINDY. *(Slips ring on; jaw drops.)* Oh, my goodness gracious. It gives my finger a whole new look.

MARVIN. Do you like it?

CINDY. It fits like a glove!

MARVIN. 'Course, it fits like a glove. Helmsley Sparks in the fine jewelry department guaranteed it would fit. He studied your finger in the lunch line three days running. Each time you'd reach for the carrots, he'd go bug-eyed behind his bifocals. You're left-handed.

CINDY. I am!

MARVIN. He promised it would fit to a tee.

CINDY. Marvin Chomsky … this is really for me?

MARVIN. Only if you'll marry me.

CINDY. Oh, I don't know about that. I like the ring—the way it sparkles—but I'd like to have it without strings attached.

MARVIN. Then it wouldn't be an engagement ring.

CINDY. Couldn't we call it a *friendship* ring and leave things as they stand?

MARVIN. But then I couldn't take you on the Super Chief with me to Las Vegas on Wednesday!

CINDY. *Super Chief? Las Vegas? Wednesday?*

MARVIN. *(Presents two train tickets.)* I bought these two months ago, right after I got my raise. See, we could be married by the weekend, honeymoon in one of those fancy gambling casinos, play the one-armed bandits, and come home broke, happy, and all spent!

CINDY. Aren't you taking a big gamble already? I mean, look— this ring, two train tickets, a hotel room, probably ....

MARVIN. Not probably. Definitely. We aren't going to be sleep- ing outside with rattlesnakes and cacti ...!

CINDY. But, Marvin ...!

MARVIN. Cindy, *The Sands*!

CINDY. Sands?

MARVIN. It's a plush casino-resort. You know, movie stars ... millionaires ... mai-tais.

CINDY. Isn't that Hawaii?

MARVIN. Well, all right— your-tais and other tais.

CINDY. Maybe a tequila sunrise!

MARVIN. Or tequila sunset! We'll have a honeymoon suite with room service day and night! They even do your wash!

CINDY. No hanging clothes on a short line over a hot oven in a cramped kitchenette.

MARVIN. No pull-down bed, either. You'll be sleeping in the lap of luxury. With me!

CINDY. *Mr. Chomsky!*

MARVIN. Imagine—fresh air—warm sun—away from this harsh Chicago weather. One week of paradise.

CINDY. But, Marvin, we haven't even had an ice cream soda together. How d'you know we'd like to share the same sunrise/sunset glass?

MARVIN. I would sip out of anything that had your mouth upon it.

(CINDY is shocked. Eyes fixed on her lips, MARVIN moves his mouth to hers. Entranced, she nearly succumbs. Hyperventilating, she breaks from him, collects toys.)

CINDY. Well, thank you, but my mouth is a little more selective!

MARVIN. Are you saying my mouth isn't appealing to you?

CINDY. No, Marvin, I'm not saying that, at all. I like your mouth. You've got a very nice mouth, as far as mouths go. But there's more to marriage than sipping out of the same ice-cream-soda glass ... *(A hurtful memory.)* ... you've got to be careful of the backwash.

(Very busy.) I mean, you've been my boss for two years now. I just never thought of you in a romantic way. *(Eyes fall on the ring.)* Something like this might take some adjustment. I mean, how do I go from saying Mr. Chomsky to Marvin-honey? I could put the wrong price tag on the Joan Crawford doll!

MARVIN. I have loved you from afar, and now I love you from a-near. I can say without the least bit of trepidation in my voice that I love you, Cindy McPherson. You're sweet and you're kind, and you work like a dog. I mean, look at you—you look like hell. *(CINDY is taken aback.)* I mean that in the kindest sense of the word. I have dreamed of this moment for twenty-four months. When I'd approach you at your vulnerable best—tired and worn down—that yellow pencil with the teeth marks implanted into wood, stuck in your head—and I mean that as a compliment! I like your hair, with all those messy curls, like a peeled onion coming apart in a stew pot. *(Wild-eyed.)* Even if you had mud caked on your face, I'd want to make jungle love to you!

CINDY. *Jungle love?!*

MARVIN. You know, like wild animals mating in an uncensored *Tarzan* movie. Normally, there's nothing wild about me. Nothing daring, or dashing, or adventurous. Why, I wear horn-rimmed glasses, my hair is slicked down with Brill Creme, and my shoes are as shiny as a baby's behind.

CINDY. And you triple-knot the laces!

MARVIN. That, too!

CINDY. Not a lace out of place!

MARVIN. No!

CINDY. When I'm down on my hands and knees picking Twidlely-Winks up off the floor, I just marvel at your knots.

MARVIN. Cindy, seeing you that first day so long ago, unchained my heart! I leaped like a leopard out of my skin. I've got a fierce tiger in me that just wants to rip off this buttoned-down shirt and charge at you like a raging rhino, and take you to my tree house like a bird of prey!

CINDY. *(Alarmed.)* You keep that tiger in your shirt!

MARVIN. It's a wild beast craving for physical attention! No! Physical exhibition! I could stand in our front-of-store display window and bellow like the Ape Man!— *(Thumps chest, does Tarzan yell.)* As I swing from window to window, all around the block, ripping off one piece of clothing after another, until finally, all one would see of me is a man in a loin cloth, cradling the woman he loves, half-naked in his arms, smacking his lips upon hers!

CINDY. Marvin, do not take your clothes off for all of Chicago to see! The windy city would be blown off its feet! This is a family department store. We sell family merchandise! Family toys! No half-naked Tarzans and Janes!

MARVIN. I want to be your toy. We'll be a Lionel Train, Tinker Toys, and an Erector Set all rolled into one.

CINDY. It's the shock of an Erector Set that worries me. I've never seen you like this before.

MARVIN. Love has made the King of the Jungle out of me. I'm ready to roar!

(MARVIN roars fiercely as he rips off his shirt, buttons popping, with tie still in place.)

CINDY. *Marvin! (Looks frantically about.)* What would Santa say?!

MARVIN. He'd say that you're his holiday gift to me! What about you?!

CINDY. I'm keeping my shirt on, thank you very much!

MARVIN. Even on our honeymoon?

CINDY. *Marvin!* You're making me blush peaches and cream!

MARVIN. *(Sits; unties shoelaces.)* Something is stirring inside of you. I know it is.

CINDY. Marvin, you're untying your triple knots! *(MARVIN tosses shoe over shoulder.)* You're tossing your shoe away! *(MARVIN peels off sock.)* You're removing your sock! *(MARVIN tosses sock away.)*

MARVIN. *(Removes second shoe and sock.)* I want to run around shoeless and sockless in the toy department! And roll up my trouser legs! *(Rolls pant legs up to knees.)* I'm the happiest beast in the jungle!

CINDY. But I haven't said yes!

MARVIN. You haven't said no! Go on! Say it! I dare you to! Say no! *(CINDY sputters.)* See?! You can't say it! *(MARVIN reaches.)* Take off your shoes!

CINDY. *No!* See I said it. I said no.

MARVIN. No, no. You said no, but not no to my marriage proposal. Yes?! Say yes!

CINDY. No!

MARVIN. *Yes!*

CINDY. I won't! I refuse! I refuse to say yes or no!

MARVIN. Why?

CINDY. Because I don't know which is which. You're confusing me, Marvin! I'm confused.

MARVIN. Imagine what our marriage would be like. Our own apartment. Eating our meals together. Swinging from the ceiling fixtures from room to room! The beating of our hearts like native drums thumping!

CINDY. I'm a salesgirl! What do I know about thumping native drums?!

MARVIN. Find out. Risk it. What has love made of you?

CINDY. I'm too tired to imagine!

MARVIN. There! You see! You just said that you loved me.

CINDY. I most certainly did not.

MARVIN. I asked what love had made of you, and you answered without pause—without hesitation—that you were too tired to even imagine.

CINDY. So?

MARVIN. You didn't say you weren't in love, or that you didn't love me. You said you were too tired to even imagine, which means - now follow me here—which means … that in the deep recesses of your pretty toy-seller mind you're ready to make a sale—you to me— satisfaction guaranteed for eternity. No discount. No refund. No more Murphy bed. The sale is final. Say you'll marry me, Cindy McPherson. Sip an ice cream soda with me. The war is over. The world is at peace. I came home alive, ready to love you. The holiday season is upon us. It could be the honeymoon season. It's the eve of a wonderful life for us. With the sales temps still on hand for another week or two, I can arrange for us to get away for a seven-day trip west. And the diamond on your finger is yours to keep—the Marshall Field's diamond in the gold setting—even if you find out the tiger in me is nothing more than a meek little kitten with illusions of grandeur. A kitten soft and warm and as tender as all get out. I'm nothing special. But if you love me back, we'll both be special. Make us special, Cindy. Make us the two most special people in Marshall Field's history, as tired and as full of muscle aches and heartaches as we are. We deserve a holiday. We deserve each other. *(On knees.)* Marry me.

CINDY. I can keep the ring forever, no matter what happens?

MARVIN. I swear on my ten-percent discount.

CINDY. I've never been asked by anyone to marry him before. Not in authentic terms.

MARVIN. Marry me.

CINDY. I'm not a spring chicken. I'm pushing twenty-five.

MARVIN. Say yes.

CINDY. I do like your mouth.

MARVIN. Forever and ever.

(MARVIN kisses her lovingly.)

CINDY. *(Touches his lips.)* Your lips are soft. Moist.

MARVIN. *(Touches hers.)* So are yours.

(They kiss again, more tenderly)

CINDY. Should we be doing this in the toy department?

MARVIN. *Yes! (CINDY kicks off one shoe.)* What're you doing?

CINDY. I'm going to run around shoeless in the toy department!

MARVIN. *Cindy!*

CINDY. *(Kicks off other shoe.)* But not barefoot! I'm keeping my nylon stockings on! And my shirt … Tarzan! *(MARVIN thumps chest, does Tarzan yell.)* Oh, what the hell! It's Christmas! *(Rips blouse open. Buttons pop.)* And you're my present to me! Thank you, Santa … wherever you are!

(CINDY leaps into his arms.)

MARVIN. *(Cradles her like Tarzan holding Jane.)* Las Vegas, here we come!

(They kiss—sweetly.)

END OF THE PLAY

Nightswim

JULIA JORDAN

Nightswim

by
Julia Jordan

premiered in August, 1998 at
Actors Theatre of Louisville

Directed by Michael Bigelow Dixon
Dramaturg: Adrien-Alice Hansel

Cast

Christina	Anja Lee
Rosie	Hiliary Douglas

Scenic Designer: Paul Owen
Costume Designer: Annalise Beckman
Lighting Designer: Eric Cope
Sound Designer: Dave Preston
Properties Designers: Ben Hohman and Mark Walston
Stage Manager: Bobbi Masters

* * * **

Nightswim *was subsequently produced in April, 2002*
at the Humana Festival of New American Plays

Directed by Rajendra Ramoon Maharaj
Dramaturg: Stephen Moulds

Cast

Rosie	Kate Umstatter
Christina	Stacy L. Mayer

Scenic Designer: Paul Owen
Costume Designer: John White
Lighting Designer: Paul Werner
Sound Designer: Colbert S. Davis IV
Properties Designer: Doc Manning
Stage Manager: Heather Fields
Assistant Stage Manager: Debra A. Freeman

CHARACTERS

CHRISTINA: seventeen years old
ROSIE: seventeen years old

Nightswim

(Lights up outside Christina's house. It is midnight and her parents are asleep. Her bedroom window on the second floor is dark. ROSIE is in the front yard.)

ROSIE. *(Whispers loudly.)* Christina. Christina!

(CHRISTINA, dressed for bed in a ratty old t-shirt and underwear, comes to the window. She has not been sleeping.)

CHRISTINA. What?
ROSIE. Come out and play
CHRISTINA. We're too old to play.
ROSIE. Wanna do something?
CHRISTINA. What?
ROSIE. I don't know, something.
CHRISTINA. Like what?
ROSIE. Wanna go climb the railroad bridge? Cross the river?
CHRISTINA. We're too old to climb the railroad bridge.
ROSIE. Go skinnydipping in the old man's pool?
CHRISTINA. He's always watching.
ROSIE. So?
CHRISTINA. It's undignified.
ROSIE. We'll go to the lake.
CHRISTINA. The police will catch us.
ROSIE. They haven't all summer.
CHRISTINA. We haven't gone all summer.
ROSIE. So they won't expect us.
CHRISTINA. It's cold.
ROSIE. That'll make the water feel warm, like swimming in velvet.

CHRISTINA. There's no lifeguard.

ROSIE. So we can swim naked.

CHRISTINA. What if we drown like the Berridges' boy? Our bodies would get caught under the weeping willow in the water. No one would find us for weeks.

ROSIE. We won't go anywhere near that tree.

CHRISTINA. But there's no lifeguard.

ROSIE. You forgot how to swim?

CHRISTINA. No.

ROSIE. Let's go.

CHRISTINA. I'm tired.

ROSIE. Skinnydipping is like resting itself.

CHRISTINA. What if that rapist with the mustache and the beady eyes is out there?

ROSIE. He's in jail.

CHRISTINA. There could be another one. Beady-eyed rapists are a dime a dozen. A copycat crazy.

ROSIE. Black water, black night. He won't even see us.

CHRISTINA. Our skin glows like 60-watt bulbs at night.

ROSIE. The water will cover us.

CHRISTINA. He'll come in after us.

ROSIE. Rapists can't swim so good.

CHRISTINA. He'll catch us on the beach.

ROSIE. You can run can't you?

CHRISTINA. He has a fast car.

ROSIE. You can hide can't you?

CHRISTINA. He carries a flashlight. He senses fear. He'll find me.

ROSIE. You can fight can't you?

CHRISTINA. He's bigger than me.

ROSIE. You can scream can't you?

CHRISTINA. No one will hear me.

ROSIE. I'll hear you. Two against one.

CHRISTINA. What if there are two of him? Or three? Or a gang of crazies hiding under the weeping willow tree waiting for us.

ROSIE. We won't go anywhere near that tree.

CHRISTINA. What if there are two?

ROSIE. What if there are none?

CHRISTINA. I can't.

ROSIE. You're scared.

CHRISTINA. Yes.

ROSIE. Admit it.

CHRISTINA. I do.

ROSIE. Say it.

CHRISTINA. I'm scared.

ROSIE. Don't be.

CHRISTINA. Why not?

ROSIE. 'Cause it's a beautiful night for a swim.

CHRISTINA. It is?

ROSIE. The water will be like swimming in black velvet because the air is cool. The lake will be all ours because everyone is locked up in sleep. We will swim naked because there is no lifeguard. And there won't be any crazies because I have a feeling. *(Beat.)* It's a beautiful night for a swim.

CHRISTINA. The police.

ROSIE. It won't be the same ones.

CHRISTINA. What if it is?

ROSIE. They change their beats.

CHRISTINA. What if they haven't.

ROSIE. That was last summer.

CHRISTINA. I saw them, a picture of them, in the paper today.

ROSIE. I saw it too.

CHRISTINA. They saved a mother's little girl. C.P.R. She called them heroes.

ROSIE. It's good they saved her girl.

CHRISTINA. Heroes.

ROSIE. They're heroes.

CHRISTINA. Heroes can do anything they want, you know. They give them the key to the city and stuff like that. They could catch us swimming naked and take our clothes and make us leave the water all naked and shine their flashlights on us and hold our clothes above their heads and laugh and say jump. You'll cry.

ROSIE. I will not cry.

CHRISTINA. I won't know what to do. I'll jump and they'll laugh and I won't know what to do. I'll jump.

ROSIE. I promise you, on my honor, I will not cry.

CHRISTINA. What will you do if those heroes come?

ROSIE. I will hide under the weeping willow branches that grace the lake.

CHRISTINA. You said we wouldn't go anywhere near that tree.

ROSIE. I'll swim to the middle of the lake and tread water until they leave.

CHRISTINA. Your legs will tire. You'll drown like the Berridges' boy.

ROSIE. I'm a strong swimmer.

CHRISTINA. They'll come in after you.

ROSIE. They won't get their uniforms wet. It'd tarnish their medals.

CHRISTINA. They could take off their medals.

ROSIE. Then they wouldn't be heroes.

CHRISTINA. They could take off their uniforms.

ROSIE. Then they wouldn't be cops.

CHRISTINA. They could take our clothes and drive away in their police car. Sirens and lights and them laughing.

ROSIE. We'll drive home naked.

CHRISTINA. Our moms will catch us.

ROSIE. They've seen us naked before.

CHRISTINA. What if it's our dads?

ROSIE. That won't happen.

CHRISTINA. What if it does? Naked? *(Beat.)* We'll be in trouble.

ROSIE. *(In a father's voice.)* 'NO MORE SKINNYDIPPING BEHIND OUR BACKS—SNEAKING AROUND—DOING WHATEVER-YOU-PLEASE—FOR YOU YOUNG LADY.'

CHRISTINA. Those are your favorite jeans they'd be driving off with. You'd never get them back.

ROSIE. I don't care.

CHRISTINA. Took you two years to break them in.

ROSIE. I'd hide them in a tree.

CHRISTINA. There's only the weeping willow.

ROSIE. I know.

CHRISTINA. They'll find our clothes again and they'll know they've got two naked girls again. And one will shine his flashlight on you and one will shine his flashlight on me. And the water that maybe was like swimming in black velvet when we were alone and moving will be cold when we're still and wondering what to do. And they will order us out and we will be naked and shivering and your tan skin will turn white and frightened. They'll see right into us. Your eyes will fix on them and you won't look at me. You won't tell me what to do and I'll be so cold. They'll say "Come on out now, girls." And the water will fall away from your body with only hands and wrists, white elbows and arms to cover you. Your arms look breakable. And I'll follow you watching the water run down your back. The flashlights will glare down our faces, down our legs. They'll shine their flashlights one for each of us. They'll smile at us trying to cover ourselves. They'll hold our clothes above their heads and smile at us naked and say "jump." And you'll cry and I'll cry and I'll jump.

ROSIE. We'll walk out of that lake like we've got nothing to be ashamed of and we'll look them right in the eye.

CHRISTINA. We won't cry?

ROSIE. We will not cry.

CHRISTINA. When they hold our clothes above their heads and won't give them back and say "Jump"?

ROSIE. We will not cry. We will not jump.

CHRISTINA. When they say with grins on their faces and our clothes in their hands, when they say ....

ROSIE. *(Cutting CHRISTINA off.)* "Lucky for you."

CHRISTINA. "Lucky for you it was just cops that found you and not some crazy sicko."

ROSIE. "Murderous peeping Tom."

CHRISTINA. "Rapist."

ROSIE. "What are you two thinking about swimming at this hour with no lifeguard?"

CHRISTINA. "What if a storm came up all of a sudden and lightning struck the lake?"

ROSIE. "Why, you would be electrocuted!"

CHRISTINA. "What are you thinking about swimming with no clothes on?"

ROSIE. "You could catch a chill and die of pneumonia!"

CHRISTINA. "It's cold at night with no sun!"

ROSIE. And when they say, "Run along home now girls."

CHRISTINA. "Before we call your parents."

ROSIE. We'll just stare at them but we won't say a word.

CHRISTINA. We won't?

ROSIE. We won't stoop to their talk, talking nonsense. We'll just press them with our knowing eyes and they'll know that we know better.

CHRISTINA. We know all about skinnydipping at midnight.

ROSIE. Warm, black water, black sky, no flashlights to trash the darkness, one moon, some stars and a weeping willow tree. A perfectly beautiful night for a swim.

CHRISTINA. Standing there naked we will not cry.

ROSIE. We will not.

CHRISTINA. I can't.

ROSIE. Why?

CHRISTINA. The floorboards creak, they'll wake up.

ROSIE. Tiptoe.

CHRISTINA. My parents have radar.

ROSIE. Climb out the window.

CHRISTINA. There's nothing to climb.

ROSIE. Jump.

CHRISTINA. It's a long way down.

ROSIE. Bend your knees when you land.

CHRISTINA. Catch me.

ROSIE. You're too old for catching.

(CHRISTINA climbs into the window frame.)

CHRISTINA. Just jump and bend my knees?

ROSIE. I don't like to swim alone.

CHRISTINA. It is a beautiful night for a swim.

ROSIE. C'MON JUMP.

(CHRISTINA jumps.
Lights out.)

<u>END OF THE PLAY</u>

Commodity

STEVE MOULDS

Commodity

by
Steve Moulds

*premiered in April, 2003 at
Actors Theatre of Louisville*

Directed by Frazier W. Marsh
Dramaturg: Claire Cox

<u>Cast</u>

Lakota	Chris Ashworth
Hunter	Dimitri Meskouris

Scenic Designer: Brenda Ellis
Costume Designer: Andrea Scott
Lighting Designer: Sandy Harned
Sound Designer: Ben Marcum
Properties Designers: Tracey Rainey and Ann Marie Werner
Stage Manager: Abigail Wright
Assistant Stage Manager: Denise Olivieri

CHARACTERS

LAKOTA
HUNTER

TIME AND PLACE

A dive bar in a crappy part of town.

Commodity

(Two men sit at a small table in a bar. Both have bottles of beer. LAKOTA, the smaller of the two men, attacks the following monologue with increasing desperation. HUNTER sits, impassive, and appears to listen.)

LAKOTA. Ultimately, this is what you have to consider—money isn't worth all that much. I was thinking about this the other day. I saw one of those billboards on the street for some credit union, or bank & trust company, something like that, and it's this huge picture of George Washington. You've probably seen it—the one dollar bill, right there, blown up really big so you can see all the little grains in the paper? And I had the thought, "They're not actually selling me the idea of money. Sure, they put a dollar bill up there on the side of a building, but wealth isn't the message. What they're selling me is George Washington. They're putting our founding father on a sign and asking me to trust him."—Do you know what I mean? Give them my money, my fifty-hour-a-week wages because George is going to watch over it personally. But what am I going to see at the end of the day? I mean, if the point of that billboard was for me to invest and make loads of money, it would've been Ben Franklin up there, not George Washington. The one dollar bill is the currency of the common man; consequently, it ain't worth all that much. And that's my biggest point. The world is full of these ways to move money around that don't get you anything but a few service fees if you might actually require speaking to a human being. You're paying the bank to hold *your* money. *You're* taking the risks on the stock market so that our economy can stay healthy. The good of the corporate giant over the good of you is what it boils down to. The question I guess I'm posing is, Does money in the hand actually translate into greater riches when the world's designed to make you spend it anyway?

(HUNTER says nothing.)

LAKOTA. Now when I say money in the hand I'm talking about *forms of currency*—bills and coins, the hard stuff, what we call cash, as if it's real and the rest of it isn't—and when I say it ain't really worth all that we think it is, I mean that on a deeper level than just saying that it's easy to part with money when there's so many ways to spend it. Actually, what I really mean to say is that currency is worth what we decide it is. Eeh? We're all partners in a grand conspiracy to give money value. Because it's paper, right? At its most basic level, the stuff is paper. The dollar is a construction. We've actually evolved, as a species, from one kind of economy, where the value of a thing could easily be set by the people involved in the transaction, to a system where men stand around a meat market talking about value and worth as if the numbers themselves were the important things. "Global Systems Networking International just went up two points." And the concept of two points means a few hundred thousand dollars to someone in a room somewhere holding onto the right pieces of paper, but to me, sitting here with you right now? I have no idea what it means. I don't even know what that company does for a living. It's the number two with a plus sign on a stock ticker while I sit here with my drink, which cost me five dollars, and five dollars is fifteen minutes of my time, when I'm getting paid anyway, and so I think, "My fifteen minutes equals this beer." But if the price of beer goes up for some reason, and there's a lot of reasons why such a thing might happen, my fifteen minutes are suddenly worth less than they used to be. But the amount of work I do, and the amount of time it takes me, hasn't changed. So it makes you wonder about a setup where the rules are changing all the time. Tell me I'm wrong if you think so, but there are times when I wonder if we wouldn't be better off trading things, bartering. Money just seems crass half of the time, especially when nothing's being bought, it's just the exchange of funds. You know what I mean?

(HUNTER says nothing.)

LAKOTA. Hell, paper money is the worst culprit of all. We're talking about a form of legal tender that after World War One was used by German citizens as wallpaper. Wallpaper, 'cause it cost more to go buy the real stuff than it did to glue up a bunch of Deutsche marks. Time was, each dollar bill guaranteed you a certain amount of gold in the Federal Reserve. I had an old bill once that said "Silver Certificate." Those two words were important. They gave you a sense of confidence, really laying it on the line what this little piece of paper meant—this thing can be cashed in for a precious metal. But dollar bills today, they say "Federal Reserve Note" on them. The idea's the same, but it's a little more insidious. It's like saying, "Oh, the government wants you to know this paper's worth something." Sure, until it's worth a little less because the government decides to print more of 'em. At the end of the day, after all the tricks the old U.S. Treasury Department can pull, a dollar might as well be ten might as well be a hundred. What's it gonna matter? In thirty years, we'll all be using five dollar bills to pay for gum balls anyway.

(There's a little bit of a pause, until it's clear that LAKOTA's finished talking.)

HUNTER. You don't have my money.
LAKOTA. Whoa, I didn't say that.
HUNTER. Yeah you did.

(Beat.)

LAKOTA. Okay, so I don't have *all* of it, no.

HUNTER. How much do you have?

LAKOTA. *On* me? Like right now?

HUNTER. Like if I hold out my hand and you were to put money in it, how much would that be?

LAKOTA. Well, it's not a lot, I'll say that.

HUNTER. *(Puts his hand on the table.)* I can count it. Only thing you have to do is put it down. *(Short pause.)* Unless you don't have any for me. Is that the case?

LAKOTA. Would that be problematic?

HUNTER. According to our deal? Yeah, that would fall somewhere within the realm of "problematic."

LAKOTA. Refresh me on this deal again. Say ... I don't pay. Then you ... what is it you do?

HUNTER. "Extract payment however I see fit."

LAKOTA. That's ... widely interpretable.

HUNTER. It's one of the reasons I loaned to you.

LAKOTA. I agreed to that?

HUNTER. You did.

LAKOTA. I must have been drunk.

HUNTER. Yup.

LAKOTA. I gotta say, I'm disappointed in you, Hunter. You took advantage of me.

HUNTER. I'm supposed to feel bad you can't keep your shit together?

LAKOTA. The very least you could do, if you're not going to help me, is look the other way. But *you* get me drunk and sign me up to some open-ended—

HUNTER. Whose idea was this loan, yours or mine? *(Pause.)* That's not rhetorical, Lakota. You're supposed to answer.

LAKOTA. ... I guess it was mine.

HUNTER. I don't feel any guilt about making a deal with you that you asked for. It's not my fault that you needed so much cash. It's not my fault that you asked me. And it's not my fault that you decided to bring liquor to the bargaining table in an attempt to butter me up. I warned you that the deal was harsh, and you took it anyway. "I still need that money, man. I'm in deep." So don't pull this guilt-trip bullshit.

LAKOTA. I thought that owing a lot of money to a friend would be better than owing money to many different people at once. You know, like a debt consolidation program.

HUNTER. Everybody else paid off then?

LAKOTA. Well... no. But you're the one I owe the most to.

HUNTER. I would hope so.

(Beat.)

LAKOTA. What's the interest if I pay you next week?

HUNTER. No.

LAKOTA. Come on, it's at least a payment plan.

HUNTER. No interest, and not next week.

LAKOTA. Okay then. I'll give you everything in my pockets—except a buck-fifty so I can get home—but the rest is yours.

HUNTER. *(Hand out.)* Okay. Do it. Then we'll talk.

(LAKOTA pulls somewhere between twenty and fifty dollars out of several different pockets—crumpled bills, nothing actually in his

wallet—not the mark of an organized man. He puts the sum in
HUNTER's hand.)

HUNTER. This is less than one percent of what you owe me.

LAKOTA. All right, so think of it as half a day's interest.

HUNTER. I already said no to the idea of interest, Lakota.

LAKOTA. What? How is that a bad thing for you? You get little bits here and there, extra pocket money for shopping excursions and whatnot. It's convenient.

HUNTER. No, it's embarrassing because it means you'll be coming around every other day with a few piece-of-shit bills in hand expecting me to be keeping track, like you'll ever be clear of it.

LAKOTA. I don't know what you want me to say. I don't have ten thousand dollars. I just don't.

HUNTER. Then maybe it's time to invoke that clause.

LAKOTA. "However you see fit"?

HUNTER. Yeah, that one.

(There is a silence as LAKOTA tries to think of something to say.)

LAKOTA. How's Willow doing?

HUNTER. She's great. We're great. Stay on topic.

LAKOTA. I can't be curious about my ex-girlfriend?

HUNTER. If you pay attention, you'll notice we're conducting business right now. What you're doing is rude.

LAKOTA. Back off, asshole. I'm just asking how she's doing.

HUNTER. I said she's great. What more do you wanna hear?

LAKOTA. I don't get it, Hunter. You're always so damn sensitive about it, but *you're* the one who took her from *me*.

HUNTER. *(Maybe he laughs.)* I didn't take her from anyone. She didn't belong to you. If she did, you woulda put up a fight, instead of what happened, which is you went and fucked her sister because you were pissed off. Then you woke up in the morning, took one look at her and started thinking about what a sad man you are. How is that going, by the way? You two still together?

LAKOTA. Yeah, pretty much.

HUNTER. Good luck with that.

LAKOTA. Fuck you.

HUNTER. *(Smiling.)* Trying to make things personal so I'll ease off the debt. We still haven't decided how I'm going to take payment.

LAKOTA. Well, you don't want to get interest, so—

HUNTER. Shh. I don't want to hear from you until I figure this out. *(Pause.)* You really think money's worthless?

LAKOTA. Obviously not.

HUNTER. No, I think you're right. I've got enough money. What do I need with a little more?

LAKOTA. *(After a hopeful moment.)* ... Are you serious? I don't have to pay you?

HUNTER. I didn't say that. No, you owe me big. Huge. I'm not letting you off.

LAKOTA. What then?

HUNTER. Here's what's going to happen. You won't give me a single dollar of your money. You won't have to pay me ten thousand dollars, now or ever, with interest or not. From now on. But I own you.

LAKOTA. What?

HUNTER. I own you now.

LAKOTA. What, uh ... does that entail, exactly?

HUNTER. I'll think of things that I want done, and then I'll ask you to do them. And you shouldn't refuse.

LAKOTA. Who are you, the mafia?

HUNTER. I'm not going to ask you to put a hit out on someone. I'm talking little things. That'll be enough. Little things.

LAKOTA. And when does the debt get paid off?

HUNTER. You owe me ten thousand dollars, Lakota. Little things don't pay that off.

LAKOTA. What if I would rather pay you all of the money than be your errand boy for life?

HUNTER. Are you ready to produce the money?

LAKOTA. No, not this second.

HUNTER. Are you ever going to have the money? Even in installments, are you ever going to put together that money? Be honest with yourself.

LAKOTA. ... No.

HUNTER. Okay then. I own you. That's how I see fit to extract payment.

LAKOTA. *(Deeply resentful.)* What's my first task?

HUNTER. Don't have one yet. You'll know when I come up with something. You might even enjoy it.

(Beat.)

LAKOTA. Can I ask you something?
HUNTER. Sure.
LAKOTA. You knew I was going to default on your loan.
HUNTER. Of course I did.
LAKOTA. Why did you do it then?

(HUNTER sincerely considers this.)

HUNTER. Because I like seeing you fail.

END OF THE PLAY

Body Talk

TANYA PALMER

Body Talk

by
Tanya Palmer

premiered in December, 1994 at
Actors Theatre of Louisville

Directed by Heidi Marshall
Dramaturg: Michelle Spencer

Cast

One	Wendy Allegaert
Two	Anita Vassdal
Three	Gina Zeiler

Scenic Designer: Paul Owen
Costume Designer: Kevin R. McLeod
Lighting Designer: Suzanne Mulder
Sound Designer: Sean Vail
Property Master: Mark J. Bissonnette
Production Stage Manager: Judy Clemens
Assistant Stage Managers: Megan Wanlass and Brad O. Hunner

CHARACTERS

ONE
TWO
THREE

Body Talk

(Images of women's bodies—female iconography. Then flesh. Maps projected onto flesh. Then bodies disappear. Lights up on three women, isolated from one another. The first woman is captured, like in a photograph.)

Exhalation

ONE. I see myself in a drugstore window. Tall. Wearing big boots that make me feel like I'm strutting everywhere I go. Supercool. Tight pants. Black. And I can't believe it's me 'cause I'm beautiful. I don't even recognize myself, and it's like a whole other individual has taken over my reflection. She's thin and she's got a big smile and she stands with her shoulders back, not crouching forward, and she looks mean through her happiness. Tough. And I love her. Love her. ME. I recognize that stupid shy scared sadness not quite ready to leave her face. And I hear her fear. What do you do when you've never liked yourself, never known how to. Always thought you were nothing good, only something to hide. But one day like magic you see yourself full of love for yourself like a spell has been cast. I see, touch, taste that face. My face. And my body and my beauty shines a beam of light so bright I'm propelled forward, down the street and into a coffee shop. I enter with my big thick boots and flash a big smile at the girl behind the counter with the cat eyes and the golden hair. She's wearing a shirt that's sea foam, that's the color—sea foam. "I love your shirt." She smiles and says "thanks" and I'm feeling so sexy, like heat just at the surface of every part of me, she can feel it too. We exchange glances like it's too bad we're in a crowded coffee shop otherwise we could rip our clothes off, except my boots, and see just how fucking amazing we are. Everyone looks up and takes me in. I smile a huge, generous, I'm-giving-you-a-piece-of-me smile to this man with graying hair sitting on a black and pink stool and he smiles back. We are radiant, the two of us together, and me and the cat-eyed girl are radiant too. I turn again and flash my smile to the whole fucking place and they smile back and I think this, Thomas Merton, is an example of universal love. This is me saying I love myself so much I can love every single one of you, that's how much love I got in me. I buy a mochaccino 'cause it's the most expensive drink, and I love this and myself and I don't need anyone else to tell me why.

Diving, Drowning, Driving

TWO. I don't know my body too well 'cause I never felt like it really belonged to me. I only floated around in it like it was a canoe, traveling with me as a passenger inside. Except I had no paddles. No control. No knowledge of how a canoe operates. How do you steer a canoe? What is a canoe made of? I didn't know it. Or know how to know it. And when you first touched me and I kissed you back and we ended up in my bed and your thin body and your tiny hips scooped me up into the center of you and traveled into the center of me and I felt comfortable and happy and I thought this is my home. Right here, that point where my body meets your body that's the place I can be I, if you see what I'm trying to say. You were hesitant, which made it even better. I tricked you into my body—that guest house I'd been crashing in for a long time, but now I'm home and I can relax and unpack. You welcome me in, your tiny hips, your curving stomach, your thin chest. I hold you against that flesh around me like a child and you crawl down and rest your head on my belly and I cry, just a little so you might not notice, 'cause you are so beautiful. Most of all *this* is so beautiful, this flesh house of connected bodies where I see myself for the first time. But it's disappearing. I know that. I pretend not to, but I do know. That day when we went out driving in the car, my car, I'm driving, you're holding the map, it's open on your lap and you're saying nothing. Nothing. I can't breathe in the silence. We're driving through the prairies and there's nothing but farmers' fields and highways and I don't know where we're going or why, so I keep trying to think of something to say, like "There's Black Diamond, that's where they make that cheese," or "What do you think they're growing in that field, do you think that's canola? My father used to call canola rape seed. I hated hearing those words coming out of his mouth." And I keep talking, and you smile at me, and sometimes you speak, but it's still silence 'cause it's not speaking to me, could be to anyone. Suddenly I know each moment we spend in silence our bodies are stepping further and further away. I can feel myself disappear. *(Lights begin to fade out.)* Your thin hips, your beautiful child's body are floating away and I try to crawl back into my canoe, but it's not there anymore, I've given it away. I look in the mirror to remind myself what I look like, but I don't recognize myself as me. What is what I like, and what is what *we* like, do you know what I mean? Do *I* like going to movies, or do *we*? Do *I* like sleeping till noon, or do *we*? Do I like making hash browns for breakfast and eating them outside on the stoop and do I like strong coffee and do I like the clothes I'm wearing and do I like my new haircut, or do We? Where do I go to feel at home now? Where did I go? Where am I? Is any of this making any sense?

THREE: I'm trying. To be positive. If I don't I start having panic attacks. Don't look alarmed. Well, I guess it is alarming. It's alarming for me too. When suddenly I start to breathe really quick and shallow. Hyperventilating. I don't always know what starts it off, it's usually nothing concrete, it's something in my head, a thought like for example "that was the stupidest fucking thing you could have said." "Idiot FAT UGLY idiot." And from that point on I lose a sense of connection to real events. "You're stupid, you can't do anything, you'll never do anything, ever. Ever. Ever." And why not? It doesn't make any sense. I'm smart. I'm … I'm what? I'm not a fucking thing. I'm a vacuous vacuum. I'm a collection of sour gases. I'm a series of mistakes. That's when I start to hyperventilate. So I'll be positive, so I don't have to put you through that. So as not to alarm you. When I was growing up I went to the Unitarian church and they taught us this chant: I am lovable and capable. So as to empower the soul. If you love yourself, then you can love others. So the theory goes. So I say that to myself. I am lovable and capable. Or I change the order. I am capable and lovable. Or I say one without the other. I am capable. But am I lovable? And I look down at my body and it's been destroyed by my mind. The sour gases turn my skin sour. It's not smooth it's scaly, it's not tight, it bursts into hideous bubbles of white fat. FAT. I want to punish this fucking body for being so fucking ugly it makes me sick so I try different things, like sometimes I hit my head against the wall over and over again until I almost pass out. Or I punch myself in the gut or I just stare at my face and scrub at it hoping I can make it disappear. My body is covered in a cloak that says to people, stay away, 'cause if you get too close I'll contaminate you with my sour gases. But then I'm lonely so I say to that face in words that slice through flesh, "You're incapable incapable incapable of making friends. No one could ever love you. You're unlovable because you're nothing but badness." So if you want to know why I'm hyperventilating it's 'cause if I didn't force myself to breathe I'd stop. My body is making one last effort to bring my mind back to life. All I can do is cry or scream 'cause that's how much I hate me. The sour juices are stewing and simmering inside. They whisper to my flesh. You have committed a terrible sin. How do I atone?

Escape

ONE. So I get in my truck and it's a stick which is so I'm in control and I'm going and I get on the road. And the black and green and beautiful yellow of the prairies is flying by me and I'm screaming inside my body "I'm leaving I'm leaving I'm leaving my home!" I let my truck say good-bye to the land that raised me. 'Cause I can't say it myself, not out loud. Suddenly my body and my truck are the same animal, both driving through the rain, skin flying past the canola fields, tires driving over asphalt. Going FAST. Claresholm where we'd always stop at the 7-Eleven for Slurpees, Fort Macleod where they roast the turkeys in a big metal torture chamber. See you NEVER. I don't want to stop, ever, ever. Only to piss or shit or pump gas. I feel ecstasy. My boots pump hard against the gas pedal, my hand grips the stick.

THREE. I lift this hand from the steering wheel for a moment and reach out the window, searching for the passing air. On the highway, the wind rushes beside my head, ear. Hands, fingers unfolding. My hand is out the window, my arm is riding the wind, floating, up and down, waving—like waves on the ocean.

TWO. Landscapes are moving past me like slides or cue cards, changes faster and faster. Mountains, lakes, pastures.

Driving through Colorado, New Mexico.

Now I'm in canyon, red rock surrounding me, above me.

THREE. Sssslipping ….

ONE. Sexy place that canyon.

TWO. Leaving Flatland. Fatherland. Homeland.

ONE. I run through ripples in the rock, feeling them beneath my skin. Rocks all around and ruins. It starts to get dark, so I stop below a canyon and put up my tent, surrounded by couples wearing hip outdoor wear and driving Jeeps. A van pulls up and three women pour out. They are wearing dresses, loose, dropping to the ground. One chain-smokes. The other listens. And the third, the tallest, watches and sees. She is the most beautiful and clearly the leader. They move around her cautiously. Gathering their gear from the back of the van, laughing, they brush against one another, looking for excuses to touch. They set up in the center of the campground, surrounded by rising red rock. As the light of the sun vanishes completely, the light of their fire rises up and with it the sound of their voices, these three women singing. Chanting. Bellowing. My friend whispers to me:

THREE. "They're witches."

ONE. Suddenly their sound takes flight. Shooting up into a beam of light, my sight paralyzed by one image—the flame and the woman, tall and beautiful, her silhouette projected onto the canyon wall, the flame licking her shadow. My body, caught in the upward motion, floats between the canyon walls and the earth. Feet, thighs, cunt, belly, flesh, tits, neck, collarbones, cheeks, eyes, hair, swept up, floating in the fragrance of their chant. My body is a part of the air, the canyon, the earth. Flesh is no longer simply flesh, it is an element that creates the earth. It takes on divinity.

The next morning the women are talking and eating, one is smoking, they laugh. But quietly. Compactly. Nothing remarkable. When I get into my truck and drive away, I carry with me my roots which travel above, below and through the earth and air which carry me. I. Feel. At home. Inside. My body. Everywhere I go.

END OF THE PLAY

Game Theory

PETER SAGAL

Game Theory

by
Peter Sagal

premiered in August, 1997 at
Actors Theatre of Louisville

Directed by Jeanine DeFalco
Dramaturg: Meghan Davis

<u>*Cast*</u>

Annie (Mark)	Gina Giambrone
Paul	Philip White

Costume Designer: Kevin R. McLeod
Lighting Designers: Michele Gallenstein and Brian Shippey
Sound Designer: Shane Rettig
Properties Designer: Mark Walston
Stage Manager: Megan L. Kelly
Assistant Stage Manager: Omar Kalal

CHARACTERS

MARK: mid twenties.
PAUL: mid thirties.

(Race and sex are flexible.)

Game Theory

(Two men in business suits, MARK, mid-20's, and PAUL, mid-30's, stand on either side of a line drawn on the ground.)

MARK. Let me see if I understand this game....

PAUL. What's to understand?

MARK. I just want to say it out loud, so we both understand.

PAUL. What's to understand?

MARK. Why don't you explain it, then?

PAUL. You have to convince me to step over the line. I have to convince you to step over the line.

MARK. Why?

PAUL. To teach us negotiating skills.

MARK. That doesn't make any sense.

PAUL. Sure it does. It's just a game.

MARK. What are the rules? Games have rules.

PAUL. No rules; just the arbitrary goals. I get you to come over to my side, you get me to come over to your side. Thus we learn the skills of negotiation and persuasion.

MARK. But it can't work. I mean, I gain nothing by going over to your side of the line. That's not negotiation, negotiation you have to offer something. Mutual benefit.

PAUL. Okay. I'll buy you lunch if you come over here.

MARK. Oh, come on.

PAUL. Really.

MARK. That's not negotiation, that's bribery.

PAUL. Like you said, there are no rules. Just results.

MARK. "You Are the Bottom Line."

PAUL. What?

MARK. The motto of the camp.

PAUL. I didn't know.

MARK. They got it written on the gate. In the grillwork.

PAUL. Come on, what do you say, huh? Step over the line, I'll buy you lunch.

MARK. How do I know that you will?

PAUL. Because I'm a nice guy. I keep my word. Ask anybody.

MARK. Nobody here to ask. Everybody else is on the Trust Tower, dangling each other on ropes.

PAUL. Then you'll just have to trust me.

MARK. Besides, getting a free lunch has got nothing to do with the game. If I cross over the line, I lose the game.

PAUL. So?

MARK. So that's the point, isn't it? Not to lose.

PAUL. I thought you thought the game didn't make any sense.

MARK. Maybe not, but that's why we're here, to play the game. There's something to learn here.

PAUL. You know my boss sent me here.

MARK. So did mine.

PAUL. My boss is very eager to see how I do.

MARK. I don't think anybody is going to grade us. This is supposed to improve our interpersonal business skills, our sense of self.

PAUL. Well, If my sense of self doesn't improve significantly, it's going to be out of a job. So what do you say?

MARK. I think you're worried too much. It's just a game. There are lessons to be learned if you win or lose.

PAUL. So let me learn from winning. Then we can share our insights.

MARK. No, wait. Let's be logical about this. What are they trying to teach us?

PAUL. To figure out how to win.

MARK. What would be the point of that?

PAUL. Winning.

MARK. Winning what? How often in business do you have to convince someone to cross a line?

PAUL. It's a metaphor.

MARK. Right. For what?

PAUL. I don't know, for quarterly sales; tell you what, I'll buy you dinner, too.

MARK. All the meals are included. Low fat and nutritious.

PAUL. Then when we get out.

MARK. We're going about this the wrong way. We've got to

think like the people who put use here. They're consultants. Corporate management consultants, right?

PAUL. Yeah.

MARK. How do they pitch this to our Vice President of Human Resources? Send us your junior execs, and for five thousand a head we'll teach them to cross lines?

PAUL. It's possible.

MARK. So the question is, how does your Human Resources veep think? An oxymoron, I know, but still. Remember when he put one of those kitten hanging from a twig posters in every single cubicle? "Hang in there?"

PAUL. What's your point?

MARK. That there's something Soft and Cuddly here. Something warm. Hidden beneath the apparent cold binary cruelty of a win-lose situation. They want to teach us something. How to think outside the lines—as it were.

PAUL. Tell you what—I'll just give you cash. Buy your own dinner when you're back in the world. Get something with cream sauce. Something with meat, for God's sake.

MARK. I don't eat meat. I like the food here.

PAUL. If you don't cross, I'll punch you. I'll tear you limb from limb!

MARK. You'd have to cross the line to get at me. And then I'd win.

PAUL. You're a lousy businessman. You couldn't sell water in a draught!

MARK. What are you doing now?

PAUL. I'm trying to provoke you into attacking me. Then you have to cross the line.

MARK. No good, I study Zaiki-chuan, it's this progressive martial art where we learn to simply ignore all attacks.

PAUL. Look—how old are you?

MARK. What does that have to do with anything?

PAUL. The game. Trust me.

MARK. Twenty-five.

PAUL. So is everybody. You're all twenty-five, twenty-six, couple of years out of college or business school. I'm thirty-five; hanging around you people I feel like Humbert Humbert.

MARK. Humbert who?

PAUL. Never mind. The thing is, you're all here to get started.

I'm here because I've tried everything else. It's my *job*, do you understand?

MARK. What is your job, by the way?

PAUL. Vice President of Human Resources.

MARK. Oh. Sorry.

PAUL. It wasn't always this way. I was like you, they put me in sales, dangled those year-end bonuses like meat on a stick and we all bayed and yapped and went at it. But I wasn't any good, you know, they gave us this crap to sell and I knew I didn't want any and I couldn't think of why anybody else would.

MARK. I see.

PAUL. No, you don't! You're young, you think anything's possible, you've always been brilliant, you've always been picked first, you think it's never going to end! But it will, it will. The last VP of Human Resources just vanished one day. Didn't even clean out his desk. They told me to take his place and I felt a cold wind. Now I sit there, and I order kitten pictures or pictures of marathon runners and sunsets, with these slogans: "Go the Distance." "Talent Is No Guarantee of Success." But what is? There aren't any posters that tell you that!

MARK. Hey—calm down, okay? It's just a game.

PAUL. It's not! It's my life! I'm sitting there one day, wondering when it's going to be my turn to vanish, and I find the brochure for this place. "Executive Boot Camp," it says. "Send your managers to our wilderness to teach them to survive in yours." And the testimonials! The skills, the confidence! Rappelling down cliffs without a care in the world! It's what I needed. I wrote up a memorandum right away.

MARK. Well—thanks. I'm really enjoying it.

PAUL. This is my last chance. Don't you see? You're young. What does it matter to you to lose this game? It's everything to me. Please. Come across the line. Let me win.

(Pause.)

MARK. That's not necessary.

PAUL. Yes it is, I just told you—

MARK. No. I mean for either one of us to win. Or lose. We can both win.

PAUL. Are you crazy? It's one line. Two sides. One winner, one loser.

MARK. Sure. That's what it looks like. But they're trying to teach us to think laterally. If the choice is apples or oranges, we're supposed to think tutti frutti.

PAUL. I don't follow.

MARK. The rules say, you win if the other person crosses the line. But they don't say only one person can win.

PAUL. You mean—

MARK. We both cross the line, at the same time. We both win.

PAUL. That doesn't happen in real life.

MARK. We don't expect it to happen. That's what they're trying to teach us. Cooperate to achieve all your goals. I can see that on a poster, can't you?

(Pause.)

PAUL. Hmm. We cross at the same time?

MARK. Exactly. Then arm in arm we go off to lunch. It's couscous with roasted chipotle peppers today; I can't wait.

(Pause.)

PAUL. This is suppose to make us better executives?

MARK. Better people. Count of three?

PAUL. Okay. I count, though.

MARK. Deal.

PAUL. One, two, three.

(PAUL crosses over. MARK takes a step but does not cross.)

MARK. Two out of three?

(Fade to black.)

END OF THE PLAY

Guilt

BILLY ARONSON

Guilt

by
Billy Aronson

premiered in April, 2003 at
Actors Theatre of Louisville

Directed by Tanya Palmer
Dramaturg: Claire Cox

Cast

Didi	Valerie Chandler
Big Guy	Justin Tolley
Thin Man	Daniel Evans
Maxine	Bobbi Lynne Scott

Scenic Designer: Brenda Ellis
Costume Designer: Andrea Scott
Lighting Designer: Hillery Makatura
Sound Designer: Ben Marcum
Properties Designers: Tracey Rainey and Ann Marie Werner
Stage Manager: Mary Ellen Riehl
Assistant Stage Manager: Denise Olivieri

GUILT

(Four chairs. BIG GUY, THIN MAN, and MAXINE wear pajamas, sit very still. DIDI wears black dress, moves around.)

DIDI. What happened. And who did it. I need to know. *(The seated three stay still.)* I know it's late. And I'm sorry. But we need to talk about it. Now. *(The three stay still.)* We all know it happened. We know that, right? *(The three stay still.)* We're not pretending nothing happened, are we? *(The three stay still.)* Are we sitting here and hoping? Is that what we're doing? Like if we don't say anything it never happened, it'll just go away? *(The three stay still.)* What did we say about responsibility? About being adults? What makes us adults? *(The three stay still.)* We're adults. Right? *(The three stay still.)* Why. Why are we adults. *(The three stay still.)* What makes us adults. *(The three stay still.)* Adults are people who ....

BIG GUY. They always close the door when they're on the toilet.

DIDI. We, not they. We're all adults, right?

BIG GUY. They always say How are you. How are you. How're YOU.

DIDI. That's right, because—

BIG GUY. They don't let their hands go all over the place when they're talking or if they move their hands it's only when they're Saying Certain Things.

DIDI. Okay....

BIG GUY. They don't—

DIDI. You keep saying They. You're an adult.

BIG GUY. They don't—

DIDI. We.

BIG GUY. They don't—

DIDI. You're an adult. Say We.

BIG GUY. We.

DIDI. Good.

BIG GUY. They don't rub their privates on things. They don't put their hands into their mouth. If they have to laugh when you're talking they don't just laugh they wait 'til you're done and then they laugh.

DIDI. Because we're considerate, right? Because, as adults, we're aware, of the other people. What they're feeling. And if we harm someone, we speak up.

THIN MAN. You can be in a room with like fifteen people. And you can tell what they're expecting, what they need to hear you say. You can anticipate their expectations. There's like a rhythm going on.

DIDI. You mean, at a party?

THIN MAN. You're surrounded with expectations but you're working within that. Who knows who from where, who wants you to say what. How to adjust your meaning, how to handle a silence, or like if there's somebody you want to get in with, how to take whatever phrase comes at you and spin it a certain way so in the blink of an eye you're— *(A fit of panting.)* you're smack in the middle of the person's— *(Violent panting.)*

DIDI. There's a breeze, it's swirling all around you, a cool breeze.

(He stops panting, sits calmly.)

THIN MAN. You're in the middle of the person's affections.

DIDI. Well, you're talking about how we're able to connect to one another, and you're right, we are connected. And if we do something that disrupts, that affects the whole community, we can't curl up inside a shell. Right? We have to, what. We have to speak up.

MAXINE. I went out by myself.

(DIDI waits.)

DIDI. Uh huh.

MAXINE. I took a shower and I went out by myself.

(DIDI waits.)

DIDI. Does this have to do with—

MAXINE. I took. This morning. I took a shower. I took a shower.

A shh... I took a shower and I went out by myself. I went out by my-self.

(DIDI waits.)

    DIDI. Does this relate to what we were talking about?

(DIDI waits.)

    MAXINE. I went out.

(DIDI waits.)

    DIDI. This is obviously very important to you, and we'll talk about it later, but right now we need to talk about how someone was killed. *(The seated three stay still.)* It's a scary word, I know. And it's sad. It's very sad, but we need to talk about it. Or it will be out of our hands, we'll lose control, of who we see every day, who we can be with—
    THIN MAN. If you kill someone, you get killed.
    DIDI. Sometimes.
    THIN MAN. When somebody's killed, they kill the killer. That's the rule.
    DIDI. But the details matter, don't they? How the killing hap-pened. What the person who did the killing was thinking.
    THIN MAN. They kill the killer. That's the rule.
    DIDI. Well I hate that rule. And I don't accept it.
    BIG GUY. I think it's good they kill the killer because that way the dying happens in pairs and nobody has to be alone.
    DIDI. That's ridiculous. *(The seated three stay still.)* Listen. There's not going to be any more killing. We're going to get to the bottom of this right now. We're going to take a trip. So close your eyes, everyone. *(THIN MAN starts panting. To THIN MAN.)* You can bring your cool breeze along on the trip. *(BIG GUY wrings his hands, whines softly. To BIG GUY.)* You can bring your song. Okay? Con-centrate on your song.
    BIG GUY. *(Spoken, not sung.)* La. La. La. Dah.

*(THIN MAN stops panting. BIG GUY stops wringing his hands and
    whining. As DIDI speaks the others rock and sway, losing them-*

selves in the imagined journey.)

DIDI. So we're drifting ... drifting off ... towards a spot ... that's sort of dark ... but familiar ... a small sore ... that you just have to touch.... You're tumbling down ... and there you are. Where are your arms. What are they doing. See exactly where you are at the moment it happened.

THIN MAN. But what if it's the kind of thing you can't ever see, even when you're in it.

DIDI. What do you mean?

THIN MAN. Like if somebody's talking, but then the channel gets changed and you're way down the hall.

BIG GUY. La la.

THIN MAN. Or there's an arrangement of people, you get all these thoughts, then the color's slipped out of everything.

BIG GUY. La la.

THIN MAN. You can't tell one minute from the next.

BIG GUY. La. Dah.

THIN MAN. And you're looking at your hands feeling lonely.

BIG GUY. La la. La la.

(MAXINE stomps her feet. BIG GUY wrings his hands, whines.)

THIN MAN. It's got to do with the head, doesn't it.

DIDI. Go on.

THIN MAN. It can't happen unless it gets to the head, that's where it always happens. *(THIN MAN places his hands on the sides of his head and stands up slowly.)* Somebody's hands were on my head.

DIDI. That's right. *(MAXINE leaps up and charges Didi's empty chair, stops herself.)* Don't stop. *(MAXINE spreads her arms like she's about to embrace the chair, charges right into it, shoves it all around the floor.)* Good. Good.

(MAXINE sinks to her knees, BIG GUY springs up.)

BIG GUY. Someone was holding my body in her arms. And I was holding her body in my arms. And my eyes got wet. And she held me harder. And her eyes got wet. And she said I'm sorry. I'm very very sorry. And I knew she was leaving me. And I thought "This is how it is to be killed. I'm being killed."

DIDI. That's right. That's it. I killed you all. *(The three sit and stay still.)* I kept seeing you struggling, and never getting better, and I couldn't take that, so I decided to quit. I wanted to tell you. But I didn't know, how to put it. So when you were resting, I went over to each of you, and held you, and walked out. I went far away and I got a new job. But I kept hearing you. In the sounds coming from a radiator. *(BIG GUY emits a short whine, sits still.)* In the breath of the person across from me. *(THIN MAN pants for an instant, sits still.)* Right now I'm at a party, aren't I. Yes. I'm at a party. The adults are saying How are you and laughing in wonderfully varied patterns. I'm listening to their stories. And I'm nodding. But I'm not with them. I'm with you. I'm seeing you, still struggling, still not getting anywhere, and I feel like you're dying, like I killed you. But we're all just born, with certain tools, and awful things strike, they just drop down, and some of us just get hit, and the rest of us just keep going. I can't change that. I can't save anyone. No one can save anyone. Why can't I accept that? Since I left you it's been twenty years. That's a life sentence. When will I be able to talk to the people who are actually in the room?

(DIDI sits.)

MAXINE. I took a shower. It was freezing cold. Outside. I walked by myself outside and it was freezing cold. I was walking. There was trucks and there was dogs. The steam coming out of the dogs. There was, coming out of my head, twigs. There was twigs coming out of my head. I was touching my head and there was twigs. There was twigs coming out of my head. The shower. It was the shower. I took a shower and I walked out. I had ice on my head. The ice was the twigs. That's what I was thinking. When they came out. When they took me back I was thinking. I have ice coming out of my head.

DIDI. So do I.

(DIDI sits still, thinking. MAXINE charges into her, hugs her. BIG GUY stands, hugs her. THIN MAN puts his hands on the sides of her head. All three stand, embracing DIDI, moving slightly, as she sits completely still looking out.)

END OF THE PLAY

More Ten-Minute Plays
from
Actors Theatre of Louisville

Edited by Michael Bigelow Dixon
Foreword by Jon Jory

Ten-Minute Plays
from
Actors Theatre of Louisville
Volume 3

Edited by Michael Bigelow Dixon and Michele Volansky
Foreword by Jon Jory

Ten-Minute Plays
from
Actors Theatre of Louisville
Volume 4

Edited by Michael Bigelow Dixon and Michele Volansky
Foreword by Jon Jory

SAMUEL FRENCH STAFF

Nate Collins
President

Ken Dingledine
Director of Operations,
Vice President

Bruce Lazarus
Executive Director,
General Counsel

Rita Maté
Director of Finance

ACCOUNTING

Lori Thimsen | Director of Licensing Compliance
Nehal Kumar | Senior Accounting Associate
Josephine Messina | Accounts Payable
Helena Mezzina | Royalty Administration
Joe Garner | Royalty Administration
Jessica Zheng | Accounts Receivable
Andy Lian | Accounts Receivable
Zoe Qiu | Accounts Receivable
Charlie Sou | Accounting Associate
Joann Mannello | Orders Administrator

BUSINESS AFFAIRS

Lysna Marzani | Director of Business Affairs
Kathryn McCumber | Business Administrator

CUSTOMER SERVICE AND LICENSING

Brad Lohrenz | Director of Licensing Development
Fred Schnitzer | Business Development Manager
Laura Lindson | Licensing Services Manager
Kim Rogers | Professional Licensing Associate
Matthew Akers | Amateur Licensing Associate
Ashley Byrne | Amateur Licensing Associate
Glenn Halcomb | Amateur Licensing Associate
Derek Hassler | Amateur Licensing Associate
Jennifer Carter | Amateur Licensing Associate
Kelly McCready | Amateur Licensing Associate
Annette Storckman | Amateur Licensing Associate
Chris Lonstrup | Outgoing Information Specialist

EDITORIAL AND PUBLICATIONS

Amy Rose Marsh | Literary Manager
Ben Coleman | Editorial Associate
Gene Sweeney | Graphic Designer
David Geer | Publications Supervisor
Charlyn Brea | Publications Associate
Tyler Mullen | Publications Associate

MARKETING

Abbie Van Nostrand | Director of Corporate
Communications
Ryan Pointer | Marketing Manager
Courtney Kochuba | Marketing Associate

OPERATIONS

Joe Ferreira | Product Development Manager
Casey McLain | Operations Supervisor
Danielle Heckman | Office Coordinator, Reception

SAMUEL FRENCH BOOKSHOP (LOS ANGELES)

Joyce Mehess | Bookstore Manager
Cory DeLair | Bookstore Buyer
Jennifer Palumbo | Customer Service Associate
Sonya Wallace | Bookstore Associate
Tim Coultas | Bookstore Associate
Monté Patterson | Bookstore Associate
Robin Hushbeck | Bookstore Associate
Alfred Contreras | Shipping & Receiving

LONDON OFFICE

Felicity Barks | Rights & Contracts Associate
Steve Blacker | Bookshop Associate
David Bray | Customer Services Associate
Zena Choi | Professional Licensing Associate
Robert Cooke | Assistant Buyer
Stephanie Dawson | Amateur Licensing Associate
Simon Ellison | Retail Sales Manager
Jason Felix | Royalty Administration
Susan Griffiths | Amateur Licensing Associate
Robert Hamilton | Amateur Licensing Associate
Lucy Hume | Publications Manager
Nasir Khan | Management Accountant
Simon Magniti | Royalty Administration
Louise Mappley | Amateur Licensing Associate
James Nicolau | Despatch Associate
Martin Phillips | Librarian
Zubayed Rahman | Despatch Associate
Steve Sanderson | Royalty Administration Supervisor
Douglas Schatz | Acting Executive Director
Roger Sheppard | I.T. Manager
Geoffrey Skinner | Company Accountant
Peter Smith | Amateur Licensing Associate
Garry Spratley | Customer Service Manager
David Webster | UK Operations Director

GET THE NAME OF YOUR CAST AND CREW IN PRINT WITH SPECIAL EDITIONS!

Special Editions are a unique, fun way to commemorate your production and RAISE MONEY.

The Samuel French Special Edition is a customized script personalized to *your* production. Your cast and crew list, photos from your production and special thanks will all appear in a Samuel French Acting Edition alongside the original text of the play.

These Special Editions are powerful fundraising tools that can be sold in your lobby or throughout your community in advance.

These books have autograph pages that make them perfect for year book memories, or gifts for relatives unable to attend the show. Family and friends will cherish this one of a kind souvenier.

Everyone will want a copy of these beautiful, personalized scripts!

ORDER YOUR COPIES TODAY!
E-MAIL SPECIALEDITIONS@SAMUELFRENCH.COM
OR CALL US AT 1-866-598-8449!